The HUNTER CHRONICLES

Rick Parent

First Edition

PAGE PUBLISHING, INC.
New York, NY

First originally published by Page Publishing, Inc. 2017

ISBN 978-1-64027-602-4 (Paperback)
ISBN 978-1-64027-603-1 (Digital)

Printed in the United States of America

HC-1: DAY ONE: LOVE AT FIRST SIGHT

It was cold, but not as cold as it was four weeks earlier. That was the worst ice storm in Oklahoma in twenty years. The tree tops were severed, and many power lines were still down. Coming home to Dallas from Oklahoma City, my wife (at the time) insisted we drive through the wildlife preserve. It was early on a Sunday morning, a partly overcast, drizzly day. We were the only customers. We had a great parking spot and were first in line to buy tickets and food for the animals. I was paying the young attendant for the goods when my wife (at the time) exclaimed, "Oh my god! Is that a baby wolf?" I looked behind the counter on the floor, and there he was. My jaw dropped. There he was, king of the canines, direct ancestry to God's creation—a baby wolf that would change my life forever. "Are you selling him? Can we buy him? How much? Do you take credit cards?" All of this spewed from my wife (at the time). All I remember is the young attendant saying, "Two hundred dollars if you have a license." Then I heard it, my voice saying, "Zero eight zero nine three four one one, and we'll take him when we finish the tour." My wife (at the time) leaped for joy. I was a hero. She was enamored with Native American folklore and history, and wolves are a big part of both. On the tour we finally arrived at the wolf pen.

That was mom, a Mexican gray, at the fence, prepared to protect her kids—by any means necessary.

Relaxing in a rare moment of sun was dad, 165 pounds of what looked husky-like, an amber-eyed and long-legged Canadian wolf.

I took this as the only record we'd have of his "brothers and sisters," all to be sold because of the small "cage."

This Hunter on day one, before he had a name.

The attendant was so excited that she had sold the first of the litter. They had been removed from the cage at two weeks because of the ice storm. They would have perished had the zoo crew not removed the kids and fed them goat's milk for the last three weeks. One had been left behind when they returned them to the parents one week earlier. That one was to be my new family member. As we left, the girl asked, "What are you going to name him?"

"Nocona, Quanah, Apache. I just have to think. I'm so happy," said my wife (at the time).

Over my dead body, I thought. *He's a Canadian Mexican American. He'll have a proper American name, if I can think of one.*

As we were driving home, it seemed so unreal. I drove and he sat on my lap. A wolf on my lap. Geez, *a wolf on my lap*! We read the receipt. The part that we focused on was "Animal Transfer License: 08093411." What? That was my driver's license! Oh God, we were in trouble. We should have taken him back, but what a cute face, but a wolf? A *big bad* wolf-to-be! What had I done?

HC 2: HUNTER'S NEW FAMILY: PACK

We got him home to my house in suburban Dallas. He wasn't as puppy-like; he was really calm and observant. Three dogs already lived here—a standard poodle, a border collie, and a dachshund. The poodle was shaken. When he smelled the new one, he started shaking and left the room and rarely interacted with him after that day. Jagger, the border collie, was so curious. He'd never seen a little one and just wagged his tail like crazy. He'd often bring a tennis ball in the room or the backyard to show off his talents. Julie, the dachshund, was the mother image. At night he'd curl up next to her and go to sleep, knowing she'd be there when he woke.

After a week of road sales, I returned to a dozen books and DVDs, all purchased so I could understand our new family member. My wife was going to guide me.

He was reserved and proper and never acted like a puppy, never wildly wagged his tail at dinnertime, never barked, whined, or howled when he wanted something. He seemed to be constantly learning. He would get most excited when I was a few minutes from arriving home. He always knew.

The picture of him below was seven days into our life together. He loved when I touched him, always leaning into my hand, and yes, he smiled. Wolves have more facial muscles than a dog, and although I didn't know that at the time, I could read him so easily.

What a beautiful boy, so fragile, so tiny, he would need a powerful name to compensate. Scout? Recon? No. Hunter. Hunter was the perfect name for my buddy. Hunter seemed to love the sound and responded immediately, somehow looking like, "It's about time you figured it out. I knew it the day I was born."

By the way, about all those books and DVDs? I can tell you now that none of them was a solid source of information. The best, most accurate for me was a Discovery Channel documentary by Jim Dutcher and his wife, Jamie, entitled *Wolves at Our Door*. The only line in the entire project that fell short was "Because of their independence, wolves make poor pets." That depends on what you want out of a pet and what you intend to offer the pet. If you want a pet that will "roll over," "sit," and "speak" when you command them, if you need that to impress your friends or yourself, *get a dog*. I can honestly say that I have had a best friend. We've played tricks on each other, consoled each other, nursed each other. Never above or below but equal and honest. Hunter and I have been amazingly close friends, deeply in love with each other and devoted to do the best for the group. Our relationship became unequalled in my life. Such a small guy, but not for long.

As a baby, Hunter was so intensely attentive.

HC 3: A TRIP TO THE PET STORE

Ready to go shopping

In Mesquite, Texas, there is a Petsmart, really a wonderful step-up from the old-time pet stores. They have grooming, training, lots of products, pet-expert employees, and they encourage you to "bring in your pet." Sounded like a perfect Sunday trip for Hunter and me. When we entered, so many people had the usual "Aah" and "Oooh" stuff, I could barely get past the turnstiles. Finally, Hunter was looking at merchandise—collars, sweaters, balls—and then his eyes lit up. A fuzzy stuffed toy. It had to be my imagination, so we tried a couple more aisles. An igloo for dogs caught his eye, Port A Pet carriers made him shake, but he kept squirming. So we returned to the first aisle, and sure enough, his tailed wagged like crazy. Okay, his first toy would be a stuffed toy duck. I picked it up and it squeaked. Hunter was amazed. As I turned, the assistant manager was standing there with an admiring look. "What a beautiful Siberian," she pronounced as she began feeling his bone structure. "Amazing, ah, bone definition. Where did you get it?"

"Oklahoma. It's a male. His name is Hunter." He looked so proud of his name. I was. No sooner had she walked off than the manager closed in. "She's new. He's obviously a malamute and beautiful. They make great pets. And you bought him a toy" This was amazing to me. Siberian? Malamute? Did they not see the rich amber eyes? Long legs and defined snout? Oh well, after all, they were the experts.

Standing in line, a little girl no more than five was captured by Hunter. "Can I pet him? Will he bite?"

"Yes and no," I said. "He's very friendly, and he seems to like you too."

"Mommy, look, a baby wolf." My jaw hit the floor. Did they know they actually did have an "expert" after all? I quickly paid for the toy—oh yes, and an igloo—and a young clerk carried the igloo to my van. I thanked him, put Hunter in, and heard the clerk mutter, "It's a damn wolf." I didn't take Hunter shopping again but filled his life with stuffed squeaky toys that he spent endless hours throwing, chasing, and squeaking.

On Monday I took him to my office. I was the boss, and only one employee would be in that day. Sharon, married to a lawyer and a *big* animal lover (her, not the lawyer), she fell in love and Hunter did too. He was now two months old, growing rapidly but still small and cute. We didn't get too much work done that morning, but Hunter had made his first friend outside the family. Maybe it was the lawyer thing, but Sharon looked so serious all of a sudden. "What happens when he bites some kid's face off? You'll get sued for everything."

"According to what I've read, there's never been a recorded wolf attack on a human," I said with confidence, all the while seeing the headlines in my mind. *The normally docile Wolf suddenly—* I was daydreaming when I heard Sharon's voice. "What about Little Red Riding Hood?" I looked over my shoulder as I left the office. "She was asking for it!"

At four months, Hunter had amazing posture.

HC 4: AMAZING GROWTH. AMAZING

Hunter didn't eat much, but he drank water like there was a drought on the horizon, between three to five gallons a day. His growth was remarkable. Here he is at eight months old. My wife, Beverley, is only five foot two, *but* he's still growing!

His look was so intense, so in control.

We had a small couch in our bedroom. When Hunter was big enough to hop up, it was his. I began wondering about what his needs would be. Food, exercise, toys, and *oh my God*, bathing. Who gives a wolf a bath? How do they do it? But it had been months, and all I could smell was that odor of a very clean pelt. When he and the other dogs played in my partially wooded yard, they would all have dirt clinging and burrs embedded—all but Hunter. His fur was like a magic coat. Nothing would stick to it, no burrs in his hair. The more I watched him, the more amazed I was. This was what God had made for our "best friend." Somewhere along the line, humans had bred and bred and inbred till they had a poodle. It reminded me of seeing the California coastline near Big Sur, the Pacific crashing into the 1,500-foot cliffs so often used in a Hitchcock movie. This, too, was one of God's creations, and Los Angeles is how we improved it—a poodle from a wolf. Great job, humans!

The overwhelming thing about Hunter was his calm. He never played with the insanity of a puppy dog. He looked as if he was babysitting when they all played. Then he would sit at my feet, his head on my foot, while I played guitar, read, or watched TV. At night, when we all retired, Hunter would observe everyone's routine, wait till we had all landed in our beds, then he would visit every dog and person in the house, ending with me. He'd give me a kiss and go to his bed for the night. I traveled a lot, and I have no real Idea what his nightly routine was like when I wasn't there. I was just told it was "different."

Justin, my stepson, brought over his new dog one Sunday. It was a yapper. The little dog was leashed to a lawn chair and just barked incessantly. Hunter just didn't get it. There was no threat, no danger, and nothing even mildly spooky, but the little guy wouldn't stop. Hunter went off and came back with his squeaky toy and laid it by the dog. He stood back, just to have the little guy continue his barking. Hunter scampered off and returned with his favorite rope, dropping it in in front of the noise machine. Nothing. Hunter scampered off again and returned with nothing—I thought. Then he leaned over by the little motor mouth and spit out a little pile of food. I was amazed at Hunter. He'd offered his toys then his food. But the little guy just sat there barking. Hunter looked at me, then at the offerings, then at the puppy. Then It happened. I wasn't sure what I was hearing. It was so low in pitch, but soon the volume was overwhelming. Hunter had growled his first growl at this little ungrateful guy. It was terrifying. Then silence. We couldn't stop laughing. The little dog gave up barking and learned how to shake.

Hunter's perplexed look

The sacred squeaky toys

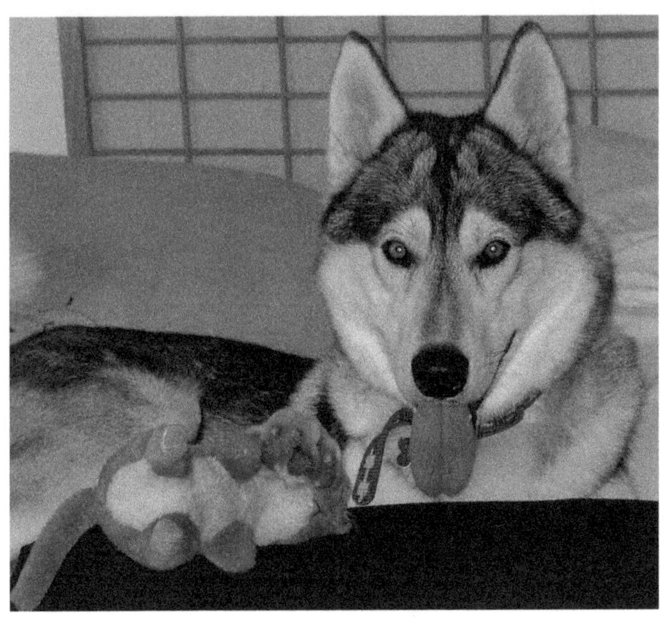

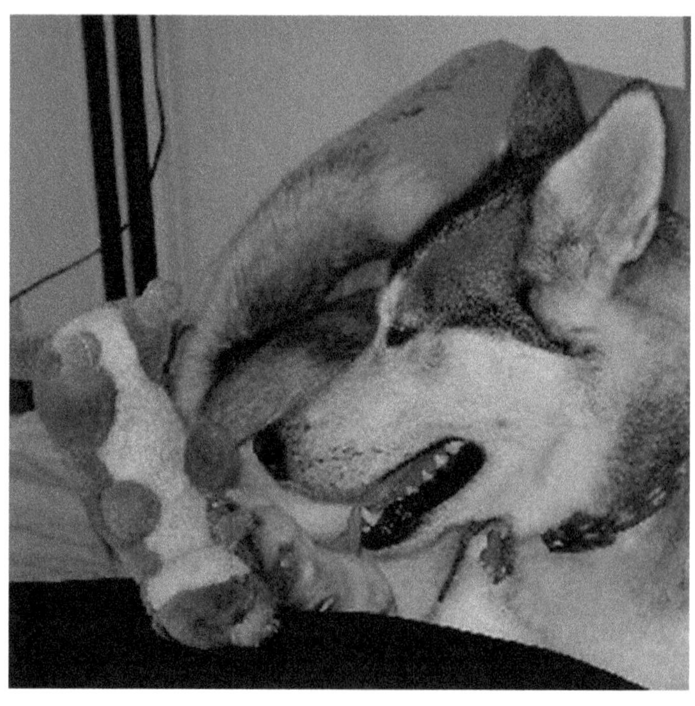

HC 5: FRANKIE AND JOHNNIE WERE LOVERS—A GREAT SONG

Hunter and Jagger were closer, but it took some getting used to. Jagger was four when Hunter came home that day, and he was the dog that admired the new member. But being a border collie, guardian of the herd from, from? Oh yeah, the foxes and wolves. He was a bit confused. He would look at Hunter then me, then Hunter again, kind of a perplexed look, kind of speaking, "He's not a dog, Dad! Look. Smell. He's *not a dog*!"

I wondered at first if Jagger would ever relax around Hunter. And he did. He, like I, fell in love with the kind and loving giant.

I thought at first it was a jealousy thing. Jagger would catch the tennis ball, return it to me, get praise for the catch, and the return. Hunter would watch and wag his tail. He would eventually get his squeaky toy, and I'd throw it, and yes, he did the Jagger thing. I just thought he was looking for the praise.

All the time they were together, they grew closer. They would often chase each other then exchange toys and chase again. Hunter could have won the game at any time, but he chose to play. He loved Jagger and never let his "brother" down. He never let Jagger go to sleep without a good-night kiss. He was a true beta wolf, the nursemaid, but beyond that he loved Jagger. All this time, unknown to me, a pack was formed by Hunter's direction, and I was privileged to be the surrogate alpha.

I just thought it would be another coming home on Friday night. Jagger wasn't there and Hunter let me know. Bev told me that he was at the vet and would come home in the morning. It was routine. It was nothing at all for me to worry about. Hunter wasn't convinced. He rarely slept anywhere except his bed, but this night it was the floor next to my side of the bed. Several kisses that night and a couple times, I woke to see Hunter sitting up, his paws and face on the bed next to me, wide awake. What was up?

Bev and her son had put a leash on Hunter, and they looked guilty as I exited the shower-and-shave portion of my morning. Bev declared, "We're taking Hunter in when we pick up Jagger." I can't print my exact words, but they weren't "Golly gee, honey, what did you do to my border collie, and where's Hunter going?"

Jagger had been neutered. I know it is the right thing for a male dog. It extends his life, prevents unwanted little ones, and calms his aggressive behavior. That is *not true* in a wolf. Only the alpha male and alpha female mate and for life and only if they know there will be enough food for the children—slightly better reasoning powers than their human counterparts. It also doesn't calm a wolf's aggressive behavior. It crushes his self-esteem. I had read all those books and watched all the DVDs. I called the vet. He agreed but had been told it was my idea. We all slept well that night. Everyone was "intact," except Jagger, and that was okay too. He'd be fine. His "pack" loved him dearly.

“The boys” playing around the pool

Playing together

Watching TV and relaxing in their usual positions

HC 6: NOTHING TO FEAR BUT FEAR ITSELF

Hunter was a little over a year old, sitting at my feet, watching the nightly news. "A Fort Worth couple is facing heavy fines tonight for owning a wolf in violation of county law." Oh my God, what was the Rockwall County Law? What did the wolf do? What should I do? "The wolf got lose, radio alerts went out, and it was finally captured by the animal control division using tranquilizer darts." The inference was strong. Okay, moms, you can let your kid play outside again. "Here's the proof that the hunt is over for this wolf." The TV then showed the chain-link cage labeled "Aggressive Animal." There, in the far back corner of the cage, was a scared and shaking wolf. The sign suddenly screamed of the prejudice against wolves. "Aggressive animal," the three pigs, Grandma or Little Red Riding Hood—who was to blame?

Aggressive animal? Pit bulls account for an average of six hundred plus attacks on humans every month in the United States. Compare that to "no known wolf attacks on a human in recorded history." One thing was a certainty: we had to keep our Hunter as much of a secret as possible. He had slipped out the front door one night, and we scoured the neighborhood for hours before I heard a rustling in the bushes three doors down. I shone the flashlight into the bushes—nothing. Then it hit me. I was stupid again but getting smarter. I shone the flashlight on my face, and Hunter came running into my arms.

The very next week, I came home to a wolf story from Bev. "You won't believe what happened when I took Hunter for a walk through the neighborhood."

"What?"

"Don't get upset. I had him on a leash and walked in the middle of the street so I could take him in any direction I wanted." What I heard was "He had me on a leash so he could drag me for miles before he headed home with my remains and walked him in the middle of the road like a *wolf on parade* so everyone could see we were harboring a 'known aggressive animal.'" It took me a while, but I finally calmed down to hear the story. A neighbor near the lake had a six-foot wrought iron fence to contain the two-hundred-pound mastiff they owned. As Hunter and Bev got within eyesight, he went nuts, barking, and finally could not control his anger and leaped clear over the fence and ran toward them. At three to four feet away from Hunter, he slowed and sniffed and rolled over, exposing his belly to Hunter, who just had a look like "Great day for a walk, eh?" Bev and Hunter walked on, and after a few moments, the big mastiff walked home, I guess a bit bewildered and possibly embarrassed. I was proud of Hunter for not fighting and played with him as Bev shopped for the dinner she planned to cook for her mom's visit that night. Chicken fried steak for six! That called for a lot of work and about eight pounds of steak, but if you've eaten it, it's a treat.

Bev opted for frozen versus fresh to save some money, and she knew she had time to defrost them in the sink. I was in my office, finishing some reports and answering e-mails from the earlier week.

Hunter was mostly with me, save a walk or two to "check on" the other members of the pack. Suddenly he walked in whimpering with the strangest look on his face. "What's wrong, big guy? Are you hurting but smiling? Weird." I held him for a few minutes and felt his nose, which was unusually wet, as was his cold face. Weird.

Then I heard the screams. "My steaks! Where is he? That [fill in any word that would mean "bad boy"]!"

I knew right then what his odd facial expression was. " Hey, Dad, have you ever eaten ice cream too fast and had a brain freeze?" I replaced the steaks and laughed, and yes, Hunter and I slept in my office that night, both very happy. Satisfied.

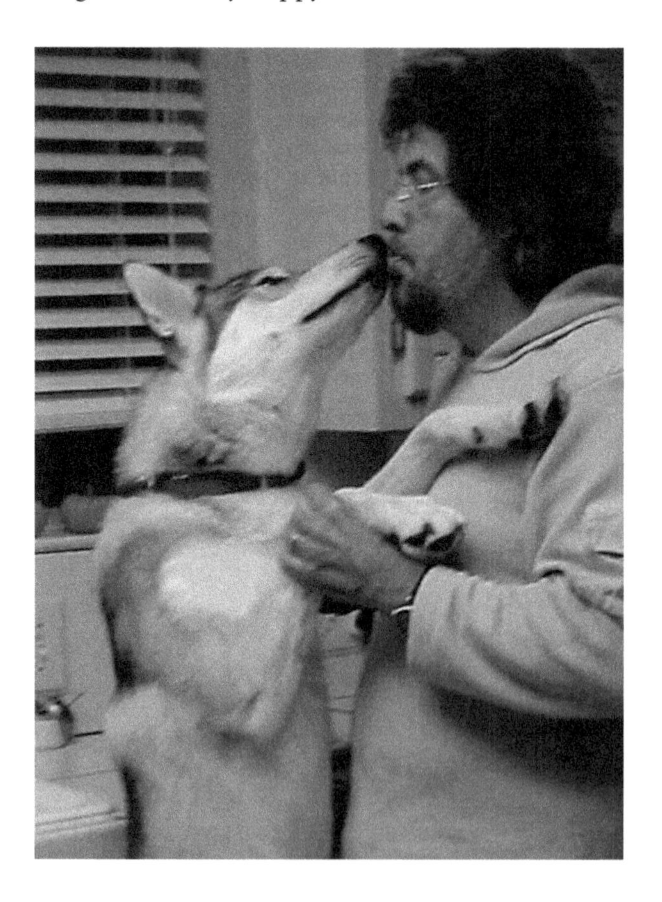

When you're this tall, the sink (lower left corner) is in your territory—easily!

HC 7: A HEART ATTACK AND THE NEED TO GIVE UP HUNTER

Pressure from all sides, they call it stress, but stress is no big deal. My company had six employees, and we represented twenty-one different manufacturers in the music industry. Beverley and I had separated, and it looked like divorce was the next step. I had to keep the sales up, employees paid, and a soon-to-be ex happy, and had to travel. The term "wolf sitter" couldn't be found in the want ads.

I had to entertain giving up Hunter. The Candy Ranch was suggested to me by Bev and several other sources. I think they are in New Mexico or Arizona, and they are a wolf-rescue group. I looked at them on the Net and just cried. I was in a bad place, and I wasn't about to face it without my best friend.

My office was on the second floor in a "stairs only" building. Halfway up the stairs, I was out of breath—*really* out of breath. So I went down to the first floor and bought a diet Coke. That's what I needed. Halfway up, I was again halted by breathlessness. I had to start working out. After a rest of several minutes, I finally reached the top. Sitting at my desk, I heard a dripping sound. A leak in the plumbing? What plumbing? I have been up in the ceiling, no plumbing. It was now dripping on a wet carpet. What was going on? It was me. Sweat water? Call it whatever. It was pouring off me, and there was a puddle around my chair. No elephant on my chest, no pain down the arm, then 911, a stretcher, then a helicopter, and the surgery. I was lucky. I urge everyone to *know* the real signs of stress-related heart attacks. We're not as tough as we think we are, and none of these parts are under warranty.

I was flown to Baylor Medical Center and the next morning, had 2 stents put in. It was all a blur for about twenty hours and then I had no worries, no fear no stress. The attending nurses were so friendly I thought they were flirting. Indeed, the truth is they were interviewing me. Most Hospitals admit you, patch you up, and send you home. That's not what happens at Baylor. They want to gather enough information to be able to tell you why you had a heart attack. After four days of this treatment, my cardiologist came to visit before I was released. "I've got a list here of eleven things for you to do to avoid a repeat of this event. If you make these changes, you can live a wonderful life for many years. If not, you will have a couple years and most likely not survive your second event."

"They" were not little changes to my life, they were very big. Get a divorce, give your company away, sell your house and move to the 100 acres you own in Commerce, Texas. It went on from there but each one he had good reasoning behind and after number five, I was fogging over. I listened to the eleven then calmly said, "No". The "suggestions" involve too many people besides me, and I can't disrupt their lives that much.

Dr. Sharp smiled and said "I understand but call me if you change your mind." Wow that was easy.

Four days after leaving the hospital, I was shuffling around in the Wal-Mart in Rockwall, not afraid to die but not sure how to live. Just then near the front of the store, the grim reaper walked up, no not a huge guy dressed in black, carrying a sickle. The reaper was a short perky red head that smiled at me and said: "Sir, are you ready to check out?" "ARE YOU READY TO CHECK OUT?"

I wasn't afraid of dying but I wasn't ready to check out! I turned away from her with what had to be a very frightened face. I reached into my wallet and called Dr. Sharp's office. He laughed and laughed and only said "That's a classic!"

I gave up my business, moved to a hundred-acre stretch of land, plopped a manufactured repo on the land, and prepared to die. But I had to work. I got a job offer while I was still in the hospital, but it entailed travel too. My friends all came through and built decks, fences, and a wolf pen, 15' × 32', more of a suite, as he and Jagger had an igloo, deck, food, water and "hot tub." They loved it. Three horses and two donkeys supplied the yard art. But I was isolated. The only neighbors were several thousand yards away, and we were the only people on a dead-end country road. I went through several "doggy hotels" in the first year, but it soon became obvious that one by one, they could not "contain" him. Eight-foot walls and fences were nothing. Strangely enough, he didn't jump to get out; he jumped to get *into* the next pen, Jagger's. My pleas went unheard, and we were banned from the places one by one. Finally, I put a notice up at the feed store and the local campus of A&M. I got a few calls, but the word *wolf* scared most off. Amazingly, my neighbors called. "Is that your note? We could spend the night there when you're gone. We love Hunter." It was a pivotal moment. I could travel without worry. Becky and Don had become heroes. Over the next years, we would become as close as family, and yes, they became members of the pack. Because I expected to die within the next two years, I had some humorous moments. "Do you want the treated or untreated lumber for your deck?" Hmmm, would it make a difference if I was dead in two years? *Big* decision! I was very alone but relaxed. Sharon, my old office manager, and I had begun a relationship. Her two boys and she had helped build decks, stairs, and fences. Her daughters were, at best, a challenge. I soon realized that kids weren't near as respectful as when I was a kid. I would have been killed for the comments they made on a daily basis. Hunter had finally stopped growing at about 115 pounds and was a very tall kisser. The horse count was soon up to seven and the donkeys fifteen and four llamas.

My life was perfect.

Sharon's 5' 7" was a perfect height for Hunter.

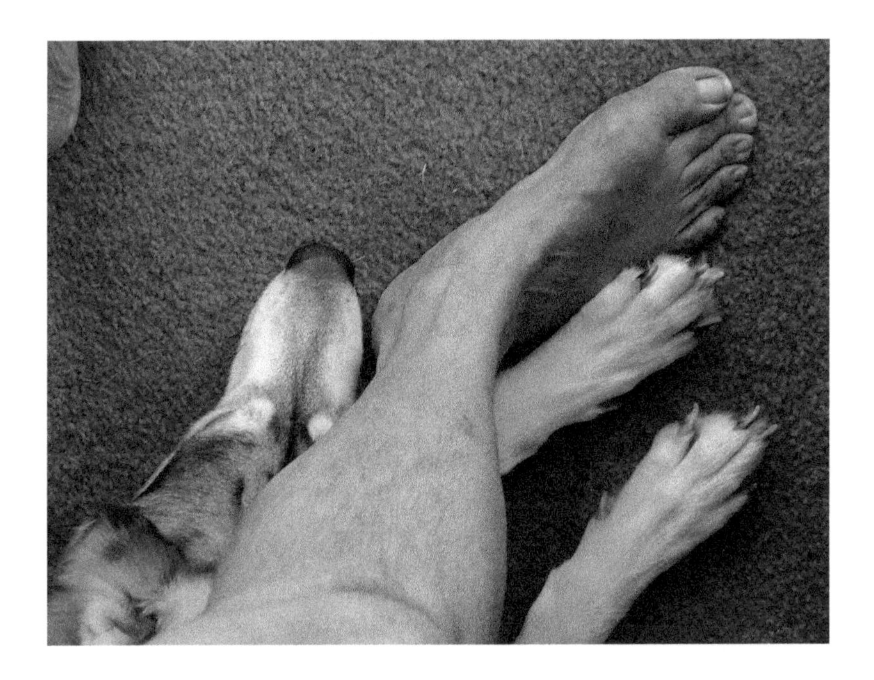

Always as near as possible, Hunter's need for contact is obvious.

Sorry, Candy Ranch. We won't be checking in!

HC 8: SIS COMES TO THE RESCUE AND LEARNS ABOUT HUNTER

My sister and I hadn't been very close. We began a pretty solid relationship when our mother died. Weird feeling when both your parents are dead, like there's no road home. When she heard of my heart attack, she packed up her daughter and headed for Dallas. She left her son and husband behind in Dublin, Ohio, to "hold down the fort." I think she was also afraid that her son might pick up some of my crazy habits—musician, divorced three times, photographer, and gun collector. Well, I wasn't what she would like to expose her son to at that time, or maybe ever. By the time she arrived, I was doing an estate sale of everything in my house and getting ready for my new country life. She wanted to stay in a motel when she arrived, "not to bother me." Huh. Five bedrooms, I was alone, she needed a motel? Hunter? She owned a large German shepherd, very loud, possessive, and aggressive. The real word I'm searching for is *scary*! Trying to remember his name now, all I can think of is Cujo. Hunter was always skittish when a newcomer arrived, and Carol was a newcomer. He stood in "the next room" with that famous half face a wolf does to increase his depth perception. Within thirty minutes, he was kissing and giving the high five, and my sis and niece were in love. She, like so many others, had a fear of the "big bad wolf." Here, the big bad wolf wanted to show off his squeaky toy. After dinner there was no need for a motel, and she loved the night check he performed before cuddling next to me on my bed. He did that for two to three weeks after the heart attack. The pack was two people larger.

Their visit really helped with the sale of so many things a person accumulates but doesn't need—actually, things that were only wanted for a fleeting moment but found a rightful place in a distant closet. If you don't know what I mean, look around your place tonight.

It was a wonderful time telling old stories while we worked the mindless chores of a pregarage sale. All the time, my niece Bonnie and Hunter were listening attentively. My heart attack had brought my sister down, but Hunter had shown us that the pack was the most important part of life. His love and constant attention to Carol and Bonnie as well as entertaining with Jagger—well, it taught us all some very strong lessons. It was August, so each day included some pool time, and Hunter loved showing off his skills of swimming, pawing the water, and prancing around the pool and yard. People often ask how I domesticated Hunter. At moments like this, and they have been many and very often, I am the student and he is the teacher.

When the two-week visit was over, Carol and Bonnie left with many pictures and more memories. Carol swore to send both her kids down for a vacation to stay at the ranch. I lost 20 percent of my heart function during the heart attack but learned to use the rest of it with a new meaning—a lot due to the love and wisdom of a wolf named Hunter.

Carol and I

Hunter relaxing

Bonnie and Hunter poolside

HC 9: HUNTER'S REACTION AND DEALING WITH HEALING

When I first learned about wolves, I realized that Hunter had assigned himself the role of the beta wolf, the nursemaid, actually somewhat of a worrier. After I had my stress-related heart attack, I was appreciative of that role in a family. Maybe it was going to save me another brush with death by stress. As I write this, I must take a second to give you a window. He is lying next to me on the couch, watching TV. I microwaved some meatballs from Walmart for dinner, and I eat one and I toss one to Hunter. I can't express the love I have for this guy, not in print, not in words, not in a poem, and not in song. He is above that. He is the embodiment of pure love.

So as a nursemaid, how'd he do? After the heart surgery, he never left my side. He calmed me with the distraction of his love. He was all over me in every way. A year later, after I had foot surgery, and yes, he was amazingly attentive. Same with a hernia operation. The day I shot myself with a nail gun, he had a different look. "You dummy" was written all over his face. But the most amazing time was his ability to "know" a time that was the worst event of my life. Thanksgiving was a wonderful holiday, actually my favorite from childhood. Sharon's family was the best group of humans ever assembled, and Thanksgiving 2006 promised to be another wonderful day. We had a lot of pilots, and Sharon's dad lived on a runway home with a hangar. His new plane was up for rides to everyone at the dinner.

Ron was his name, but *perfect* was his earning—the nicest, warmest man I ever met. He and I flew the new "kite." He laughed as I said, "I guess I should be asking for your daughter's hand." He just quipped, "You take all of her or nothing." A jog in the stick and we both looked at each other. "WTF was that?" I said.

"Not a problem," said Ron. "I had my annual yesterday, so nothing can be wrong." Sharon flew next then her youngest son, Alec. Ron and Alec crashed eight minutes later, and we found them seven hours later, both dead. I spent the night in tears with a great family and called my neighbors to take care of Hunter and Jagger for the night.

The next morning, I dropped Sharon off at her house to get the clothes she would need for the next few days. I raced to the ranch and was so angry when I reached the ranch.

Hunter was howling. I could hear him at the gate. What was wrong? I ran into the house and then to his pen. His usual jumping wasn't there. He hugged me and cried, as if like when he had been hurt. I pressed on his flesh to see where he had been bruised. He wasn't, but he kept crying. I was slow again, but I soon realized that he knew. He knew that the woman I loved, that he loved, had lost her father and her son. That's what a wolf is like. That's what living with the greatest animal in the world is like. I can not make the words any more descriptive.

I love Hunter, and he lives for and loves "the pack." That day, the pack had been reduced by two, and they will always be missed.

N115SE
11/23/2006

VOX

HC 10: NO ONE SHOULD BE AFRAID ON HALLOWEEN

The first Halloween I remember was a party, dunking for apples, and bottles of Pepsi and Coke. The diet drink wasn't invented because no one was fat. I was a baseball player, and one beautiful girl was a gypsy. She was seven years old and I was five. Over the years, things had changed, and the streetlights weren't a reminder to get home. Well, my first Halloween in the country was rapidly approaching. What was the deal? What was I to expect? Just because I lived a life that seemed to be slower and more "retro," were the times really more "back then"?

Why did it mean so much to me? Was it because I had suffered a heart attack in late July? Was I wanting to live all the parts of my life that I hadn't? The answer is, we'll never know why I looked so intently at the costumes that pre-Halloween season 2002, but I did. Maybe I wanted to dress up the child I never had. Wait, I have a child. His name is Hunter!

Well, I spent an hour looking for a costume for a wolf. Nuts? Yes!

I found a perfect outfit in the Walmart collection of fashion. He would love it, and if anyone came to the ranch, they would think him a perfect host. He wouldn't be a wolf. He'd be a loving, non-threatening, costume-wearing being.

I purchased his costume and hoped that Jagger wouldn't be jealous. After all, he was a dog, and everyone loves a dog—as a dog. Hunter was a wolf, and he would wear a costume for Halloween. He would be—a duck.

I know the photo is huge, but I wanted to show his expression. It's a loving, "What are you thinking?" look. I took the picture, removed the costume from my loving, "cooperative" friend, and no kids showed up. The candy was eaten by Hunter, Jagger, and the trash can, and I remembered a time long ago when kids laughed at the joy of a few treats, an apple bobbing, and a beautiful girl in a gypsy costume. No wolves were ever involved in Halloween (except the dreaded werewolf), and Hunter knew that. Halloween was never celebrated at the ranch again. He sat around for days and looked at me like I had betrayed his trust. I had just crossed the line, and in a brief moment, I thought him a pet and not an equal. I would never do that again, but that was right after a heart attack, and I'll use that as an excuse till the day I die. I'm sorry, Hunter. No more costumes, ever.

Here are two post scripts:

The gypsy girl and I reconnected in 2009, and her daughter got us VIP spaces to watch SST-129 lift off from the Cape. It is still one of my favorite photographs that I've taken.

I was cleaning out my cabinets in 2012, and as usual, I had Hunter by my side. He loves "helping" as much as he can. I reached way back in the cabinets in the living room and pulled out—the duck outfit! Well, Hunter not only left my side, he also ran outside and paced on the back deck. After I recovered from sidesplitting laughter, I went outside, and Hunter and I just had a great visit.

Did Dad really do that to me?

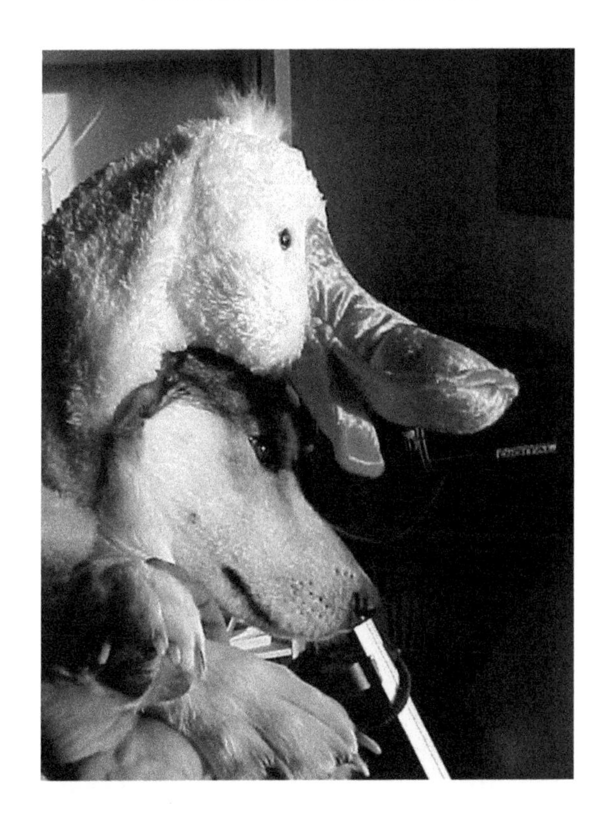

HC 11: ESCAPE: ALONE AND IN HARM'S WAY

A drunk at a party once yelled at me, "You have that wolf trapped. He's a wild animal and needs to run and hunt and kill, and someday he'll kill you in revenge for ruining his life. He hates you. He's a wolf, you idiot!" I walked away and said over my shoulder, "And I'm the alpha."

I don't let Hunter run because in East Texas, and actually a lot of the country, a wolf is fair game now, taken off the endangered species list, and often mistaken at a distance as a coyote. I had nightmares, a green-toothed redneck leveling a gun and saying, "I'm going to shoot me a wolf." At least twice a month, I would dream this. I was so afraid for him.

The third year I was at the ranch, I left the house to go to the back fields and feed the horses. I was in the jeep, and as I approached the horses and donkeys, Hunter was standing with them, wagging his tail. He had left the house somehow and run through the woods as I drove around them and beat me to the horses. They were nervous; after all, Hunter is a wolf. But he was running side to side and having a great time. I tried for over an hour to catch him—not going to happen. Then he just ran off. I watched him for several hundred yards, and I could "see" the redneck leveling the rifle. By the time I got to the house, I could barely see for tears. Walking up the stairs of the deck, I learned a huge lesson. Glass was everywhere! I had left the blinds up, and Hunter had seen me drive off in the jeep. A wolf's biggest fear is being alone, and Hunter wanted no part of that. Leaping through the window was his answer.

The country isn't like a neighborhood. A "block" can be five to ten miles around. After two more hours of hunting and hoping to no avail, I went home and called Sharon. "He's gone. He can run three hundred miles in a day. He's gone." All she said was "I'll be there first thing in the morning. Just hang on till then."

I left the picket fence gate open and the front door open also. Hope is a hurtful mistress.

I told a very stressed Jagger that Hunter was gone but that we had enjoyed his time and that was all that mattered

Jagger jumped up at 4:15 a.m., and I leaped out of bed. I could hear the rain pouring down and, off in the distance, the yipping of a wolf "playing" with the donkeys.

I grabbed the 3 billion candlepower floodlight and hit the deck running. There were the eyes of a wolf reflecting at the tree line three hundred yards away. I ran to the open picket fence gate. Hunter was racing home. He stopped dead about one hundred feet away, and I remembered when he was lost in the old neighborhood and I shone the light on my face. He ran by me and headed through the house door. I yelled out loud, "Hunter's home." More subdued, I added, "And he's met a friend." The stench of skunk was overwhelming. I didn't care. I hugged his slimy body with all my soul. When Sharon called at 5:00 a.m. and said, "I'm on the way. Are you all right?" All I said was "Yes! He's home, and stop at Walmart and buy four to five large cans of tomato juice." The silence was only a few seconds, but then the laughter was so real and so honest. She knew.

Well, one of my original questions was, how do you bathe a wolf? Answer: You don't. You shower with him. It was an unreal experience and a memory that will live forever. Sharon grabbed my camera but had a hard time shooting photographs and laughing as hard as she was. At the end of the day, he had that clean-pelt smell again, and I had earned my Native American name: Showers with Wolves.

Yes, he's trying to turn off the water!

This was a great reunion, and I'm so glad he made it through the night to shower with me!

HC 12: HUNTER LOVES PEOPLE, BUT OTHER ANIMALS?

When he first came home, Hunter was in a large "pack." I was married to Beverley, she had three sons, and I had Jagger, a border Collie while she had a standard poodle and a dachshund. So he was surrounded with a pack and very happy. But Beverley was given a love for animals and that grew to acquiring *more*.

Horses and donkeys: Hunter just saw the horses and donkeys from the van or Jeep. We stabled them fifteen minutes away from our house in Rockwall, Texas. We had a strange life, but it was a good life. Beverley had taught me that all animals, not just dogs, had personality. We would be at the stables every night we were home. Hunter watched intently but would never go too nuts till he was at the ranch. Then he would occasionally Hop over the six-foot privacy fence and "play" with the horses, but the horses never knew he was playing. He chased the donkeys a lot. Then I noticed that as they got tired and slowed down, so would Hunter. I realized that he didn't want to catch them, just chase them.

A prairie Dog: Beverley loved animals of all types, and soon we had finches and, of course, a prairie dog. I think I earned my cool badge by not saying "*What?* A prairie dog? No way!" We bought a sphere that he would enter, and he would "run anywhere" with total impunity. Hunter was amazed. This little guy in a ball, running around, and you can't, well, eat him? That never occurred to me till now. Weird. He (the prairie dog) was protected by the sphere. I should have tried to protect him from Bev. She insisted that he be "fixed." Why? I don't know because it usually takes two to tango.

But I learned really early in that marriage that you could be right or you could be happy. So I chose happy, and the prairie dog died from complications.

Sugar glider: We (Bev and I) went to a gun show. A sugar glider is a strange little guy, kind of a flying squirrel but not, very small, $150 and more for the cage, food, etc. And the last thing the salesmen said was "Don't upset him." I turned, $225 lighter in the wallet, and said, "What?" He just had a straight face and said "They have weak hearts and can't be upset, stressed, or scared. They'll die."

So I come home, and the sugar glider is in the guest room, in a special cage for his solitude and peace. Beverley would spend a few hours a day playing with this little creature. A week later, I came home off the road. I called for Bev and got no answer. I searched the rooms with Hunter, and when we get to the guest room, I see Bev with the little guy in her hand. Hunter walks in and smiles at him, close, real close. *Eeeeehehehehe*. The little guy dies of a heart attack! *No* more sugar gliders and another night in my office with Hunter. Anyone need a cage?

Skunks: After his first encounter, Hunter must have worked up a different approach, because I've found four dead skunks in the backyard—and no "Showers with Wolf."

Possums: If they are dumb enough to come in the backyard, they're dead. I was walking Hunter to the pen one morning, and a possum reared its head. Hunter took three long steps in a second and tore the possum's throat out with one swipe of his paw. Then, walking away, he looked over his shoulder at the body. It reminded me of Hurricane Carter. Weird.

Badass dogs: My neighbor Becky had a dog named Buttkiss (I know). Anyway, he was a killer and protected the chickens, etc. He had killed three of Becky's Chihuahuas in the first four months of 2005. Hunter got loose and wandered up to Becky's Place. Buttkiss started shaking and rolled over, exposing his underbelly. When I got there, Becky had Hunter on a leash, and she couldn't stop laughing at Buttkiss. Something about a wolf.

HC 13: HUNTER'S LOVE OF VEHICLES AND WATCHING THE ANIMALS

I thought Hunter would like to ride in the jeep with me as I fed the horses and donkeys. He was amazed at the transportation. Actually, I was a bit afraid he might just jump through the jeep's soft cover. He would watch as the horses came up to the jeep or as they ran beside us to the feed troughs.

Hunter was so intense. He looked like a military scout searching the land for some dreaded foe. At times I had to just stop driving and laugh and hug him. Later when I acquired an old F-250 (1987), I felt better about "closer" encounters, and as seen in the photographs, he would exchange "sniffs" with the horses through the windows. We went out at least once a week. Hunter would hear the sound of his leash being picked up and start jumping and spinning. I guess he was harboring too much energy for just a jump. Then there was the day—or should I say the night—Hunter and I sat on the back deck as we often did, him leaning against me and both of us gazing at the East Texas night stars. Maybe it was the little-boy spirit that never leaves the soul of a man. Maybe it was Hunter's idea, or maybe it was that second glass of wine.

"Let's go find the animals!" I pronounced, and Hunter was beside himself. A night field trip! A subdued howl emitted from him. He often did this when he got extremely excited. I grabbed the leash, and we headed for the '87 Ford. I started the pickup and turned on the headlights. It was pitch-black dark, and I needed all the help I could get seeing. I drove about three hundred yards to the bridge I built the year before and looked over at Hunter. He was squinting.

Weird. We traveled another four hundred yards and I saw the horses. Heading that way, I looked over to see Hunter still squinting, so as I approached, I turned off the headlights. He wagged his tail and stared at the horses and donkeys as they slowly approached. I turned on the lights to see how close they had gotten, and he looked at me like, "What's Wrong?" I killed the lights and let the interactions take place as the "dumb human" tried to make sense of it all.

He could see perfectly well in the pitch dark. I couldn't. When I had the lights on, I could see, but he was irritated by the headlights. Hmmm. A challenge. I liked challenges.

The government sells the "used" military night vision gear to optics companies (domestic only, as the technology is very restricted.) One such company is STANO. They refurbish the units and sell them to SWAT teams, crime watch, etc. The owner of the company loved my story, and soon I had a Generation III set of the real things. Night vision goggles right back from Iraq!

I never turned on the headlights again when we ventured out, and Hunter and I could see on an equal level, better than the horses and donkeys. We had many an evening, and until now I never told anyone about it. A few people knew I had the NV equipment, but no one knew *our little secret.* Hunter and I spent many a night together on walks and drives around the one hundred acres that I named Rancho Rico.

Turk and Blare out for a walk. No one is stabled here.

Hunter on patrol in the jeep

In the old F-250, he was protected.

Close encounters were a lot safer and controlled.

On the ready—for who knows what?

The only other option was sunglasses.
But Hunter rarely wears them.

HC-14: WHERE DOES THE BETA WOLF TURN WHEN HE'S HURT?

Where does the beta wolf turn when he's hurt?

We rarely get any snow here in East Texas, so it's quite a treat when we do. Really, the only snow I like is the kind that's gone in the morning. Even though Hunter's dad was from Alberta, Canada, he hates the cold too. He's a cross between an inside dog and a wimp. He was fascinated by his first look at snow and the idea that the flakes float down and he could taste them.

He and Jagger shared this love of the wintertime. They might stay out five minutes and then come in and recover by a fire or on the couch.

Almost every return to the house was accentuated by a sneeze, almost a "Bah, humbug!"

Still boys at heart, they would run and play after each other for those few minutes that they did "venture out to the Texas tundra." Not knowing how to behave in the ice and snow, Hunter ran in circles as I tried to hit him with a snowball. Jagger would try to "catch" the snowballs like his favorite tennis ball. He would stand there afterward, looking like "Where did the ball go?"

Well, when Hunter had had his fill of running and dodging, he leaped full force onto the deck. His feet landed and flew into the air. He twisted and tried to land gracefully but crashed down on his hip. It was an immediate yelp then a howl. As he lay there, trying to get up, I feared a broken hip. I was about forty feet away and covered that distance almost as fast as Hunter would have.

I crouched down next to him. He buried his head into my neck and cried and cried. I slowly pressed on his hurt hip, and the sobbing increased. I was pretty sure we had a problem, but at no point of pressing did he yelp. He just cried and cried and kissed me then would "rebury" his head on me and cry some more. After fifteen minutes of alternatively crying and kissing, I was ready for the walking test. I got up and retreated a few feet, not far just a test of his legs and hips. He slowly reached me but very cautiously, all the while whining. Some more loving and hugging and another test, each more successful than the previous.

Finally, he was okay to come inside and lie on his bed. A big, deep breath and the crisis was over. He was shaken up but intact physically. The big guy had never felt the pain of an injury. What a character he was. The love and attention was always given by him, and now he needed it in return—a first but not the last. He's been stung by mahogany wasps and caught "cat scratch fever" from a bobcat that wandered into the backyard. Painful for Hunter but fatal for the bobcat. Other than that, he's never shown any signs of being in pain or sick. I guess his most common disruption would be—spoiled. That's not only my fault but the fault of most everyone he encounters. As a matter of fact, the only person who didn't fall in with love him and that Hunter didn't warm up to was a sales manager from Behringer named Mark, a truly obnoxious character who was here on business. I tried everything, but Hunter just never got near him, and Mark was happy with that.

At one point I said, "Hey, I've got a great game that will be a perfect ice breaker for you two." I went to the kitchen, followed by Mark, and poured Ketchup into a bowl and added a little water. "What's that for?" Mark questioned. "I'm going to hide it in my mouth, and you pretend to hit me with the chair. I'll spit it out and we'll see how Hunter reacts!" Not only did Mark not want to play that game, but he locked his bedroom door that night. What a party pooper!

HUNTER

HC 15: NIGHT GAMES—BULLYING OR RESPECT

So many people have said: "Hunter's going to love me because I love dogs." But who doesn't love dogs? Wolves are afraid of humans in general. My mom used to tell us stories of walking home from school and wolves were watching her from the woods. "I kept them away by singing 'Who's Afraid of the Big Bad Wolf.' They knew I wasn't afraid, so they didn't attack." *Mom!*

They were watching, yes, but if they had wanted to attack, well, I wouldn't be here. Playing with Hunter is funny because he really plays hard. Catch the flying squeaky toy and run full force around the yard and through the house. Sometimes I'd hide and jump out. Bad move. His force and strength would just knock me down and leave me in a different place. Sometime we'd be boxing or wrestling, and my reading glasses would fly off and he would stop and look so sorry. I'd have to initiate the "game" again before he would recover. In the suburbs we had a bedroom door handle that was really a handle, not a knob. Two seconds and Hunter was in. Sliding glass doors would have to be locked. Actually, he would look to see if the latch lock was "unlocked" before opening the door.

When I moved to the country, I had two large doors installed, a slider for the bedroom going to the back deck and french doors (with round handles) from the kitchen area out to the front deck.

Hunter came and went through the bedroom door. He was so happy and free, often waking at 3:00 a.m. and wanting to "mark his territory" or look at the stars. He had no restrictions, no hours. He was a free wolf.

I am a light sleeper, and when the sliding door opened or Hunter moaned as he got out of bed, I knew it and I ritualistically looked at the clock. Twenty minutes later, he'd come in the door. In the winter I'd then get up and close the door, something Hunter never learned. Cold is bad.

On schedule, one summer night, Hunter opened the door an walked out at 3:00 a.m. At 3:40 a.m., I glanced at the clock and faced the ceiling. Did he get out? Three forty-five. Nothing. Three fifty-two and I got up to the sounds of whimpering. In the dark I lit one outdoor light, twenty-five watts. Over the laundry room, I could see Hunter running back and forth, frustrated and upset. What was wrong? I headed for the door. *Knock, knock.* What was that? I listened and heard it again. *Knock, knock.* I must have been imagining it. *Knock, knock.* Oh my God! Hunter was nuts about it. What was happening? I shook my sleepy head and focused on the direction. The sound was coming from just outside the fence on the right side of the yard. It had to be a burglar or a home invader trying to attract then drug the "wolf" that stood in the way of a successful night of plunder.

I quickly had a weapon and flashlight for the encounter. I hadn't turned on the front porch light, so my exit wasn't obvious. I slipped stealthily out the front, down the deck steps, through the picket gate, then to the outside right of the fence and—confrontation. My heart was filled with excitement. Why? I was prepared and ready for the demons of the night. As I approached, I again heard the noise. *Knock, knock!* "Suddenly there came a tapping… Quoth the Raven 'Nevermore.'" My mind raced as the thrill of it all filled me. I spun around the corner of the fence and leveled the gun and flashlight.

There, in the bright light of the flashlight, stood three horses and two donkeys, peering through the spaces between the fence slats—at Hunter. One of them, Turk, his hoof hitting a two by four that I had left on the ground. *Knock, knock.* They all froze and stared at the beam of light. They reminded me of kids caught smoking in the boys' room. They dispersed, and I finally got Hunter to return to bed. Animal tricks? Yep, just good clean fun. I smiled and dozed off to sleep.

Blair and Turk, two of the jokers!

Snowy and mom, Tinker.

Hunter's always on the lookout.

HC 16: LITTLE THINGS THAT YOU DO MAKE ME KNOW I'M IN LOVE WITH YOU

I'd just like to talk about a few things that Hunter does. Things that bolster my deep love for him. The first is the most recent—he comments by action. I read a book one time titled *Conversations with God*. What an arrogant title. But the author won me over with the first question and answer. "Why don't you talk to us?" "Why would I restrict myself to words?"

Wow, what a statement!

Hunter must have read that book. He is such a teacher and communicator. Here they are:

1. I belong to the songwriters' group here in Commerce, Texas. We perform two songs each month at the Cowhill coffee house. Well, when you live in a small college town, you always have an audience, and being a performer, I like to warm up my voice before "going on." I do so by singing at home with a karaoke machine. I sang two songs with Hunter watching me from my bedroom, relaxed and happy. Then, as I started the third song, he got off the bed, grabbed a squeaky toy and laid next to me, head on my left foot. As I started the next song, he returned to the bed. I was amused but left for the coffee house. It bothered me, and soon I returned to "duplicate" the event. Again he laid his head on my foot during one special song, "Love Me

Tender." Why? Was it the many times that Elvis said the word *love*, the same word I say to Hunter all the time? I'll never know for sure, but I do believe it was.

2. Today, as I write this, Hunter walked out on the front porch, donkeys in sight, but he just stood there, and as I said, "Hey, buddy, let's go inside," he turned and just walked in the house, choosing to be at home rather than "chase donkeys" for the next hour. Was he getting old or getting wise? I don't know, but he wouldn't have done that four years ago.
3. After a heart attack, you have to exercise, no ifs, ands, or buts. You at least walk thirty minutes a day. So I bought a treadmill and I set it for 4 mph, and I walk one hour a day. This day was a cold one and I hate the cold, so I set a fire going in the fireplace and started on the treadmill. Hunter had left his blue monkey squeaky toy right in front of the fireplace. I walked a few minutes and Hunter slept on in my bedroom. Then the crackle of the fire or the noise of the treadmill woke him. He walked into the living room, saw me on the treadmill and the fire roaring, then he looked at the blue monkey. He ran to it and grabbed it. As he walked by the treadmill, I swear he gave me a dirty look! I had to stop walking for a few to ingest what had happened. He was worried about the blue monkey getting burned! I know him well enough to say with confidence, he was worried and mad at me. You can't make this stuff up!
4. Whenever I went out front to feed the horses and donkeys or mow the front lawn or just fence mend, Hunter would watch me out the window. As I came closer, he would pretend that he was watching something else. He'd pretend he wasn't interested in me at all, but his eyes would give him away. Then when I was opening the door, he would run to me and cover me with kisses and hugs. He has a complex personality that goes so far beyond that of a dog. Sorry, but that's the way it is.

5. I don't know where it came from or who said it first, but the expression "Wolf it down" was hardly a stranger in my family as a child, but it's been the dogs in my life that ate so fast, you wonder if they tasted it. Hunter gently takes the food offered and slowly eats it. And by the way, my dogs—and I'm sure most—growl when you approach their food. Hunter just looks like he's waiting for the ketchup! I can take a beef rib from him and hand it back, no issues.

Well, those are a few of my favorite things, things I would have never experienced without Hunter.

Pretending not to care, Hunter and the blue monkey

Hunter and his squeaky duck

Hunter and I starting another day at the ranch

HC 17: HE JUST KEEPS CHASING HORSES. HOW'S HE GETTING OUT? HOW DO I STOP HIM?

You've already heard my concerns about Hunter being out alone, getting shot, getting ganged up on by coyotes. I always wondered why moms were protective. I don't anymore.

I was sure that the six-foot fence was a big-enough obstacle. After all, it was a straight vertical jump. It could have been dug under. Hmm, that would provide me a challenge. I was working in my office (the third bedroom) when I saw the horses run by the window. Playing? Running now in the other direction. Playing? I walked to the front door, wondering as I moved, where was Hunter? He was at my feet a minute or two ago. I glanced out the kitchen window. Oh my God, he was chasing everyone. I got to the front door as the "herd" was heading for the woods, Hunter at the tail. As they disappeared into the thick woods, I was worried about the horses and donkeys; they must have been scared. They didn't know that Hunter was just playing. Then a minute or two later, Hunter came running out of the dense foliage—being chased by the horses? Was this a game? He didn't have a game face on him. They were in hot pursuit. He ran the three-hundred-yard distance to the front fence in record time, hopped through the barbed wire, and turned to view his pursuers. I was there and put his leash on. I walked him to the nearest fence point, tied him to a tree, and got a vehicle to transport him to the house. I didn't need the stress of a confrontation between a wolf and a bunch of horses!

I walked the perimeter of the backyard, no tunnels, no escape opportunities. So I set up a situation. I would watch Hunter as he escaped, and he did. He walked calmly to the fence and leaped vertically right over. What legs! One motion and he was on top of the fence then down the other side. I had a challenge. I put him in the pen and headed for the feed store.

They did provide a lot of choices. It would have to be a hot wire, 5,000 volts on top of the fence. I would add a two-foot challenge to the leap and a strong reminder of "bad boy." I was reminded of the a scene in the 1956 movie *Forbidden Planet.* Hmmm, what was the problem? Keeping the monster of the id out. I saw that movie as a child, and now I was keeping the wolf I loved "in." Weird. And Hunter watched, and I could read his thoughts. "Those little wires aren't going to work."

It took a little thought. Ground in the center, hot wires above and below, shielding, etc., but in a few hours, I was ready to let Hunter out of the pen. I would fake being busy mowing the lawn as I watched with peripheral vision.

I started the lawn mower as Hunter paced along the new addition. Then he squatted down on his haunches. He lifted off the ground like a rocket. I wanted to cheer for his magnificent power, but as he reached the top of the fence, he stuck his nose and head out to confront the flimsy new wires. *Crack* and a yelp! Hunter was down and, for lack of a better word, pooping. He just couldn't imagine that a flimsy little wire could do that! That reaction went on for a couple frustrating days, then he and his body calmed down.

He looked at the fence "topping" the wall many times after that but never again tried to leap. I turned the "hot wires" off years ago. Never again was it needed.

HC 18: THOSE EARLY RANCH DAYS AND A WAR WE WON

It was the last time that I used a "doggie hotel" for Hunter and Jagger. I was on an extended business and pleasure trip and got home too late to get the kids before the "pet hotel" closed for the night.

Oh well, if that's the worst thing that happens today, it'll be a great day. I walked in the house and closed the door of my dwelling that hadn't been occupied for ten nights. *Scratch, scratch.* "What was that? A mouse, no doubt. I'll get a trap tomorrow." *Scratch, scratch.* Wow! That's weird. It sounded like that came from a different place. *Scratch, scratch.* No way. I went to bed with my eyes drooping and quickly forgot the— *Scratch, scratch.* No more games of "hide and squeak."

It was 11:10 p.m. At 1:18 a.m. I opened my eyes. *Sniff, sniff.* What? That new sound was right at my ear, and something was pricking my skin all over. Mice were sniffing my ears, and their feet were clawing into my skin. I'd say about thirty of them. I levitated to the ceiling, throwing mice as I rose. It was a Hitchcock nightmare. I don't care who's reading this. Hey! Macho man, you would have freaked too! I landed on two feet and grabbed my clothes, shook them out, and put them on!

I headed for Walmart and the pest department. They had twenty-two, four packs of mouse traps, and I added a jar of peanut butter. The kid at the checkout might have said something funny had I not looked like Jack Nicholson in *The Shining*. I armed the traps and added the peanut butter, and as I set down the sixteenth trap, the first one snapped. I laughed a sick laugh. Was this how Jack the

Ripper felt? I've gone nuts! No! *They* made me this way. They had covered my body, and I was in defense mode. By morning the count was 18–0, and I was getting reinforcements soon. Hunter and Jagger were ready and informed by the time we returned home. One big mouse ran toward me in the kitchen (away from Hunter). I kicked the mouse in the air toward Hunter, and Hunter leaped and caught him like a line drive to the short stop. He never ate the "captured" mouse, though wolves often live on field mice in the wild. He would "carry" them to the back deck and spit them out. Most died of fright long before the spitting part. Think about that. So would I; so would you! After several days of combat, we had regained our house and the feeling of control. But I will never forget the battle of the rodents and the combat leader named Hunter. It was humorous to watch this huge animal chase small invaders and have him capture them and spit them out. He didn't want to hurt them, just expel them from "the den," our home, the place where we cuddled, played, relaxed, and watched TV, and Hunter would never allow an invader—never. It was a really weird event, and I was so glad when it was over. People actually get cats to keep mice at a minimum, but I hate cats.

HC 19: DO WOLVES LAUGH?

The evening was beautiful and the horses and donkeys had headed for the back fields after sunset. Maybe it was to catch the last rays of the sunset, as those open fields face west. This was, after years, their routine. The night vision was a great addition to the ranch. If coyotes were approaching, I could see them. If the horses, donkeys, or llamas wandered back when I was walking Hunter at night, I could see them coming way off and head Hunter home. ATVs, the pickup, and the jeep took on a whole new life.

This night was going to be dark, a no-moon night. It was a great night for night vision and a walk with Hunter on a leash and Jagger running free. This made Hunter a bit jealous, but he knew it was best for everyone involved.

We walked across the first "front thirty" acres then into the woods. Hunter stopped as we neared the creek bed. His head was facing a large pecan tree, and as I peered in that direction, I smiled. A family of raccoons was playing and hadn't noticed our approach. Jagger lagged behind, smelling everything, so Hunter and I just watched the "kids" running all around the parents, and occasionally, an adult (probably mom) would swat one of the kids. Hunter would wag his tail and now and then look at me for my reaction.

Then the Jagger (a mere dog) tramped up to us in the woods like he was wearing snowshoes, and the party was over. The raccoons hightailed it, and the three of us headed back to the house, Jagger just looking like, "What'd I do?"

Soon he realized that we were heading back and started running in big circles again. Hunter had had a great adventure observing the raccoons, so he was just pacing me and happy to be out and about.

Light clouds hid some stars but not enough to matter. As a side note, the Generation III night vision allows you to see the infrared stars as well as the white light ones. There are a thousand times as many infrared stars as white light. So I'm mostly looking up and walking in wonder of God's creation. There is such a "carpet of stars" that I think that there's no room for another star, not one.

There I am in paradise, walking side by side with a wolf, my best friend, and my dog, a border collie, is running blindly through the night.

My one hundred acres has four ponds, a must for the horses, llamas, and donkeys to live a natural life. One is close to the house, very close to where our return path was.

A huge splash distracted my attention from the stars. What was that? A giant fish? A whale? A land shark? No, it was Jagger, running like there was no tomorrow and not seeing near as well as Hunter or myself (with the night vision). He had run full force into the pond and was shocked! He surfaced, then ran out and started shaking off the surprise water. Hunter stopped dead in his tracks. You know the way a puppy wags his tail so hard that he loses balance and often falls down? Well, that's what Hunter did. He wagged so hard that he lost his balance and had to sit down. I was stunned by his reaction to Jagger's mistake. He was—was he? Was he laughing?

Oh my God, wolves laugh. Yes, they do, and so did I. That dark night on the ranch, we all returned to the house and slept well, a little grin on the faces of two of us.

HC 20: JUST HOW SMART DO YOU NEED TO BE TO OUTSMART?

Outsmart is an expression that no one challenges. "Yeah! I outsmarted him" But how often do you actually see someone outsmarted?

The way my life is, it's pretty damn simple. I travel three to four days a week to see music dealers, and the remainder of the week, I try to fix their problems during an "office day." Well, I don't have an office, so that means that for eight to twelve hours a day, I sit hunched over a laptop in my living room. The good news is that I can see the backyard and Hunter and Jagger come and go as they please. Unannounced kisses, hugs, and belly rubs are intertwined with e-mails, Excel files, and Word documents.

It was a warm and sunny fall day. Hunter was sunning in the middle of the yard; Jagger sat at my feet. A sudden jump or jerk by Hunter attracted my attention. Had he heard something, seen some threat? Then I saw it—a mockingbird swooped down and pecked his head. Hunter was under attack from nature's airborne division. Hunter stood at the ready, watching the bird flying around the backyard. As the bird approached, this time I was convinced that the young flyer had overestimated his abilities. Hunter was actually standing up, paws in a defensive position. The mockingbird flew a quick maneuver and hit Hunter's head from behind. Hunter was Sonny Liston, the bird Ali (Cassius Clay back then). That one didn't go well for Sonny.

The bird sat on the fence and gloated for a moment. Hunter was intent and thinking of his best defense against this winged attacker. He was thinking more than I would have believed. As the bird approached, Hunter made his move and ran into his pen. The bird followed, and as fast as he could, Hunter ran out of the pen, slammed the door, and wagged his tail. The bird wasn't trapped, but it was shaken up. It stayed in the pen for a couple moments then flew out the back way. It didn't return, maybe because it couldn't be sure what Hunter's next move might be.

I was astonished again at the thought-process capability that Hunter processed. I was also thinking that it was a good move for God to deny wolves the opposable thumb.

That weekend was the first Monday of the month. In East Texas, that means the largest flea market in the world takes place. I don't really know how many acres it is, but it's huge and you really can't walk or shop it all in one day. Some people stay in local (Canton, Texas) motels or camp for the event. I go a couple times a year to find unique Christmas and birthday gifts. I hate shopping, but this is a "You can't tell what's around the corner" event. I'm a guy, so the giant display of pillow cases shouldn't have attracted my attention,. but it did and I smiled, glowed really. A pillow for little boys that loved to go hunting with their dads, white with letters in camouflage print—Hunter. When I got home and changed his pillow slip, I was nearly laughing out loud. I turned and Hunter, watching intently, seemed to be smiling at me. Slowly wagging his tail, he hopped up on his bed and I wondered. I've wondered a lot living with Hunter.

HUNTER
11/13/2006

HC 21: DOG LOVERS AND THE MILITARY'S NEW GENERATION OF MEN

Many people have been by to visit Hunter. Often they use the excuse of business or coming to see me, but I know better. Hunter's the draw.

The typical visit is by a dog lover. Why? If you don't like dogs, I probably wouldn't allow you to visit in the first place. Shortly after "acquiring" Hunter, I noticed how he approached people. He was timid and intently observing the new visitor to see if he picked up any signs of aggression. Usually, after about twenty minutes of distant observing from as many angles as possible, he would approach and kiss the visitor's left hand. If there was no reaction from the visitor, he would circle again and observe for a few minutes. Then he would casually walk up from the left side and lie down, placing his head on the left foot of the visitor. That was the defining moment. Right then, the visitor was the newest member of the pack.

It was a ritual that had been repeated well over a hundred times. I quickly began explaining to people what would happen, and they were amazed at the accuracy of the story. There were exceptions. The exceptions were the most fun for me. One day Ryan, Beverley's son, had a schoolmate over to study. I noticed that my constant sidekick was suddenly missing from my side. I looked around and Beverley suggested that he might be in Ryan's room upstairs. No way! It's too confining for Hunter with a stranger present. I walked upstairs and looked in Ryan's room. I was astonished. Ryan and this girl were sitting, books open, and Hunter was lying across the girl as she pet his head. "Now that's freaky," I exclaimed, and the girl just smiled, saying, "He must be able to read my mind." "You don't understand how unusual this is," I pronounced. "No, really," she said. "My mom's always making me close the door to my room when her friends visit." What?

"My bedroom walls have over a thousand pictures of wolves pinned up." Maybe, maybe he could.

I slowly walked downstairs, confused.

He has accepted all but two visitors over the last eleven years into the pack, and I agreed on both cases. The people were not worthy of his friendship. As another tidbit of observation, he plays differently with everybody, but when they return, he steps right back into "that style." He is different when he and I are alone or with Jagger. He walks closer, rubs against me more, and kisses for no reason at the strangest times. We often sit on the porch at night, and he leans against me. We stare at the sky and he sniffs the air.

There is a group of people that has had a nearly identical, shockingly warm reception from Hunter—the military, three Airforce, two Marines. These five had immediate kisses and hugs from Hunter. No warm-up time for the troops. Hunters loves 'em—Sharon's dad, thirty-five years in USAF, and her son an A-10 repairman who served in Afghanistan. Hunter was their buddy right away. Alex served in Iraq and was greeted with hugs as he entered the front door!

Kyle was Hunter's friend and couldn't or wouldn't believe that Hunter was normally timid. Kyle had completed his first of two tours in Iraq. But the funniest reaction and lecture was when Phil visited from California after three tours in Iraq as a .50-caliber machine gunner on the rear of a Hummer.

On the way to the house, Phil kept expressing how excited he was to meet Hunter. He loved dogs, especially big ones, and Hunter would love him too. I warned him not to set the bar too high and explained the "ritual." I told Phil to stand at my bedroom doorway to the living room and let Hunter show him how him how he opens sliding glass doors. I told him not to react as Hunter would most likely run by him toward the kitchen. He always knows when I've been shopping. Well, that scenario and the ritual stories went right out the window when Hunter got inside. He took three huge steps toward Phil, put his arms around Phil's neck, and kissed away! I was so shocked! This was the most enthusiastic reception Hunter had ever displayed to a new visitor. I exclaimed, "Wow, that's so cool. He really loves you!" Phil just stood there and hugged Hunter back and rubbed him, and finally, Hunter broke the embrace. Phil was grinning but shaking a bit. Then he softly spoke. "Maybe so, but that tongue is surrounded by some huge teeth. There was a moment." That was a fun night, and after a good meal and some deep talk, the subject turned to the battles. Phil is a great man, one of the new Marines that really care about and love their country. He's also human. Tears streamed down his face as he recalled losing his best friend in battle, and Hunter hopped up on the couch and kissed his face again.

The newest member of the pack was hurting, and Hunter felt his pain.

I thought you'd like to know that.

Hunter observing a new visitor

Hunter and Phil

More kisses for Phil.

Alex Played with the horses too.

Hunter never stopped playing with Kyle.

Oh yeah, the teeth!

HC 22: DOES HE HATE THE DONKEYS? I DON'T THINK SO

Since I moved to the ranch, the biggest concern has always been Hunter's safety, and when he's loose, he can run three hundred miles in a day. Wow, so I have to make the executive decision that he needs to be in a controlled area. I don't want to restrict him, but I have to. He knows not the danger that lurks. Humans can be ugly.

So when Hunter just walks out the door and runs off, I always fainted. "He's gone forever." No, he's just having a fun moment, and he just wants to come home to the pack and eat his dinner and sleep in his bed, next to Dad and Jagger.

So what's the deal when he "escapes" and chases the donkeys? Let's take a real look. I finally learned to relax when Hunter "jumped the fence" or "ran out of the door" and "got loose."

I calmed down one day and said, "He always comes home, and I should just get some great picture of him in the wild. The muscles, the stride, the physical shock of a real wolf—wow. *But* as he began to catch up to the donkeys, he slowed up. He didn't want to catch them. He wouldn't know what to do. He just loved the game. On the other hand, you can see Travis's face (one of my donkeys), and he doesn't think this is a game. He'd try to stay alive and still be the protectorate. Too funny for me. Hunter played the "game" for under an hour, maybe forty-five minutes, and cooled his feet in the pond. I stood at the edge of the pond, and with his eye peering down, Hunter walked out of the pond and onto the leash for the walk back to the house, an occasional look at the donkeys like, "See you next time." And next time if he caught them, he'd wonder what to do. He has no violence in him. Or does he?

I've had a hundred friends spend the night with a wolf, and they all spoke so highly.

"What a great lover." "He's so peaceful." "What a great animal." "I never expected him to be so loving so quickly." *But* I will also add that I have offered this proposition to everyone that has stayed at he ranch.

"Hey! Let's have you hit me with a chair and I'll spit out ketchup like it's blood. Let's see what Hunter does? Yep! You guessed it. No one has taken up the challenge and played the "game."

I can't blame them. I love them and I love Hunter.

By the way, I've often wondered, how would Hunter act? How would he react if he knew that the beef ribs he loves every night I'm home, what would he do if he knew where they came from? Hmmm, do donkey ribs taste that bad?

HC 23: WATCHING TV—I DON'T WANT TO MISS ANYTHING

Hunter always liked to sit with his head on my foot and face the TV. That was in the day of the twenty-five-inch-tube TV. He always liked being next to me in the same room, but I never thought he cared about what channel was on or who was winning the game.

I personally had been so confused by salespeople in too many stores. Then, on a day when I was way ahead of schedule, I visited the Circuit City in Plano to kill some time. The young "kid" approached and I bristled. "Do you have any questions?

"No, I'm just looking at the HDTVs. Just doing research for, you know, someday."

"Well, where do you live? What price range are you in? Is fifty-two inches the right size for your living room?"

"Yeah, it'd be perfect, but I have no way to get it home."

"We deliver."

"Not to the Gaza strip!" I said.

"No, but what's your zip?" God, the TV looked great, like 3D and bigger than the movie screen when I was a kid. Wow. "Sorry, we don't deliver to Commerce, Texas." I knew that was coming. I was in the country to "get away," and that has its advantages, but it also has the isolation factor. "What would it take to get you to buy this today?"

"Hello? Delivery and setup today!"

"Let me call Bob. The delivery guys are here and finished for the day… Bob, can you do me a favor and follow a guy home with his new HDTV?" This guy was good. "What? Bob said yes? *Yes!*"

I wanted it. In a few hours, they hooked it up and the picture was amazing. Then they called Direct TV and it got better. *Now* it was on an HD channel. The guys left and I was in heaven. Hunter! He had been penned up in his "suite," howling and jumping for me. I ran and let Hunter and Jagger loose. They ran in and smelled everything. Cardboard, plastic, extra cables—and the new HDTV.

I poured a glass of wine and turned around. Hunter was on the couch, sitting and staring. I walked around the couch and sat next to Hunter. "Is that cool, buddy?" He looked at me and howled then wagged away then howled. He was—no, I had to be crazy. Wolves have the ability to see what dogs cannot. I grabbed the Jim Dutcher DVD *Wolves at our Door*. Hunter and I spent the next forty minutes in heaven. He was so intent, looking, staring at the images of wolves and forests and trees. He was so happy. I thought for a second that he was lonely, but I put on *Pirates of the Caribbean* and he was captured. He loved the HDTV. He just kept watching, watching whatever I put on.

We finally found the boxing channel. I love boxing. It can end at any second, so you can't look away. You can't wait till the two minutes' warning and suddenly pay attention like with football or basketball.

I got another glass of wine at the rest between rounds. Hunter was with me, but the next round, he went for a drink of water between rounds by himself and was back on the couch by the bell! Weird. He didn't want to miss anything either. I was just happy I hadn't missed the chance to live with him.

Always time for tickles and grins. Never miss a punch in boxing!

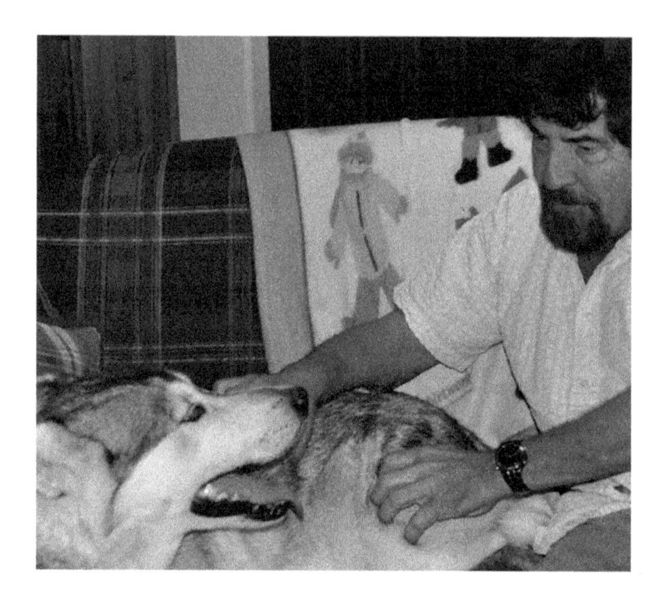

Sneaking from behind doesn't work with Hunter
A "hug or two" between rounds

HC 24: SHARON BUYS A BED CHEST, AND HUNTER IS SO HAPPY ABOUT IT

I really get upset when I hear how people perceive wolves. *Racist* is the ugly word of the day, but look at what that really means. Judging someone based on very little information, the color of their skin, whatever that is. "Oh, I really hate sitting next to green men when I eat." It sure sounds stupid, doesn't it? I just got an e-mail today—a picture of a woman with the wolf she'd murdered. She justified it because the pack was "really big" and "closing in on their cabin" and "overrunning our states." The full e-mail and photo is attached. It sickened me. Now that you know Hunter as well as you do, read her justification of the kill. Had she killed the alpha male leader? The alpha female, his wife (they mate for life)? The beta wolf, assigned to caring for everyone? Or possibly the omega that ate last and always had to submit?

Was Refrigerator Perry, the football player, a bad guy? Did he have to be shot because he was big? Are the Chinese "bad" and need to be shot because there are so many of them?

We often make judgments before we really know all the facts. It can be the cause of a really ugly moment, but in this case, it was the cause of a very funny sight and a lot of laughs. Join me and laugh.

Several Christmases ago, Sharon bought a bed chest for my bed. After we brought it in and placed it, we poured a glass of wine, exchanged stories of the week, and started to cook a supper. Hunter came in, hugged Sharon often, and played with Jagger. He also played with his squeaky toys as usual. It was a typical night at the ranch. After the dinner and dishes were done, we sat at the table, and that's when we began to think without reason.

"Oh, oh," Sharon said. "It just hit me that I bought leather for you. Do you think Hunter will react negatively to the leather? His paws are huge, and when he plays, he will shred it."

She had some good points, and I had seen him seemingly "fly" to my bed, bounce off, and fly out the door. Returning through the door, he would bounce off the bed and be in the living room in one bound. His paws were nearly the size of my hands, and his claws were quite—efficient. I had no leather furniture, so that, too, was an unknown. A wolf's sense of smell was way better than a dog's—any dog.

Well, we then walked into my bedroom to look at ways of "protecting" my new furniture. Our jaws hit the floor, then we laughed at what we were looking at. Then we laughed at ourselves for judging Hunter even when we thought we knew him. We didn't. He had taken all his squeaky toys and laid them on the new chest. He loved the new place Sharon had purchased for his toys. He wagged his tail and looked for approval of his arrangement. While we ate, he had checked out the new addition and decided it was for him (self-centered?).

Even to this day, he will occasionally redo the toy arrangement on the chest. Each time is as funny as the first. Our preconceived notions of what would happen were based on—nothing. This was another great lesson from Hunter to us, me especially. Don't rush to judgment or conclude without all the information. When we do this, we are in need of a wolf lesson.

So a couple guys were "treed" at the campground. I've played with Hunter. His strength and speed are amazing. If the wolves wanted those guys dead, I can tell you, they'd be dead. I hope that someday, somehow, these "Hunter chronicles" get into the hands of Heidi Leavitt (the woman in the e-mail.) I hope she feels some regret for the murder she committed.

The bed chest—oops, I mean the squeaky-toy home

Hunter and the duck toy

His paws are more like fingers than a dog's

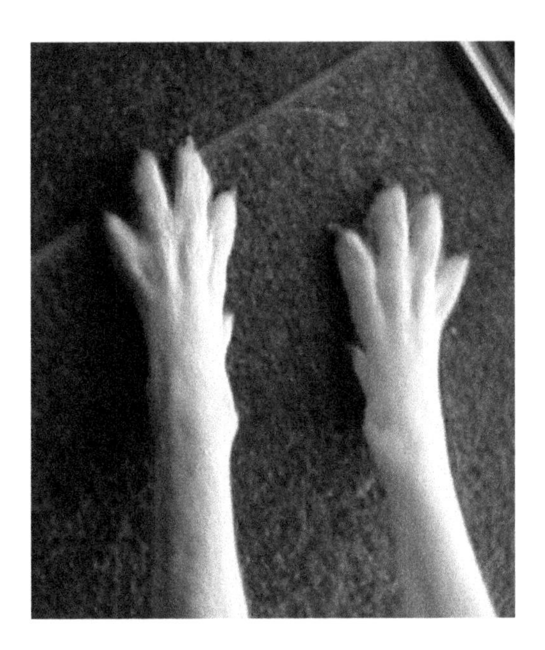

Actual e-mail :

This wolf was shot in the Salmon area of Idaho.
This is one BIG Wolf....

This is what we are up against in Idaho, Montana, Wyoming and Oregon, These big wolves are expanding their territory faster than we can keep track of them. Who is afraid of the "Big Bad Wolf?" Those wolves don't bother anything or anybody??? Guess again. Wendy who sent me this one lives near Challis.

Heidi Leavitt shot this wolf just outside their home down river at Spring Creek. Heidi was in the store and said that they have had a pack running around their place and decided when they heard about them coming their way again, they would try and shoot one (she did have a tag). So the next time came quickly and while waiting for the pack to get closer, they looked in the woods below them and there was this wolf.He weighed 127 lbs and was a collared wolf and by the time they got it to Fish & Game (which is probably an 1.5 hr drive, Fish & Game already knew about the wolf and said they had been looking for him. He is now skinned and hanging at their place.

The wolf pack had been terrorizing campers lately. Had a couple of guys treed in the cab of their pickup all night at Colson Creek campground. Not afraid of human campsites at all.

HC 25: MORE LITTLE THINGS

I've had a lot of people ask me for more short stories about Hunter, so here goes:

1. Catch-scratch fever: No, it's not just a song from Ted Nugent; it's real and very painful. I came back from a three-day trip, and Becky left me a note. "Hunter's limping but he's just a wimp. He killed a cat in the backyard and he's been acting like a baby ever since" This was a logical deduction except that Hunter rarely, if ever gave in to aches etc. I walked into the backyard to let Hunter and Jagger out of the "suite," and I about jumped out of my skin. The dead cat was lying in the yard and it was huge. I don't know about cats, but he wasn't a tomcat size, not puma size, but in the middle on the bigger side. I called Becky. "The cat's still here?" She laughed. "I wanted you to get the whole scoop!" Well, I disposed of the cat as I did all dead animals, and dragged it to the near creek bed, and the coyotes would have it gone by morning. But Hunter was really hurting, and I was at the vet first thing in the morning. Gary looked serious. "We'll try one of several antibiotics that work on [he named the medical term for cat-scratch fever; don't ask me if it was English]. If we get lucky, he'll show improvement. If there's no improvement in six days, we'll switch to another till we get the right one." I asked about Hunter being a wimp. "The infection heads for the nearest joint and festers, and no, he's not a wimp. This stuff is crippling! We don't find the right

vaccine and he'll die." It was my turn to be the wimp. I pampered him and cried for him and he just hurt. He slept on my bed. I cooked ribs and let him eat them on the carpet—because. Well, we got lucky, and in three days, Hunter was running around. But he had seven more days of meds, and we did great.

2. Hunter never begs at the table, but he's never far. When he hears words like, "I'm through," he moves closer and you wonder, "Does he know what I said?" Well, I had a pretty big party for my friends, a typical Texas barbecue, and Hunter was enjoying all the people (he had met most before). Julia, a five-year-old, was eating her chicken dinner at the table, and some of us were laughing at the way he had followed her a lot and seemed to be her guardian. He was nearby when she exclaimed, "I'm full! I can't finish the chicken." He immediately came to her rescue and made sure Mom wouldn't scold her for leaving leftovers when the kids in China… You know the story. We all laughed as he ate the remaining food then smiled at her. He hadn't stolen the food; he'd saved Julia from being embarrassed!
3. We have many "walking" scenarios at the ranch but on of the funniest was when I first moved there and Sharon's son Quinn was out. When I was looking for a house sitter but needed to travel, Quinn would spend the couple days at the ranch. One of these days, he took Hunter and Jagger for a walk. Quinn held Hunter on a leash, and Jagger was running loose. They were in the back fifty acres and walking by the creek. Although Quinn carried a pistol, he never got it out for this encounter. He was laughing too hard. Jagger was about a hundred feet in front when a coyote leaped out of the creek bed to attack. Quinn was startled but held firm on to Hunter's leash. The coyote, in midair, looked to his left and saw Hunter. Quinn said he had a look on his face as if to say, "My god! His big brother *is a wolf*!" When the coyote's front paws landed, he changed direction to *away*! Quinn watched him run for

hundreds of yards, never looking back. We laughed a lot about that story.

4. We've all been tempted by the *big doggy bone* in the pet store or grocery store. I think it's a cow femur, and it looks great being eaten by a Chihuahua or similarly small dog—David and Goliath. When other dogs eat it, it's a joy to watch. However, as I looked at the picture of Hunter with it, I couldn't help asking, "Is the UPS man missing?"

For this and all of the Hunter chronicles, I wish you'd been there.

Hunter, in pain from the attack. Even his bone feast wouldn't ease the pain.

He wasn't putting any weight on his right paw.
Neither was the dead whatever it was.

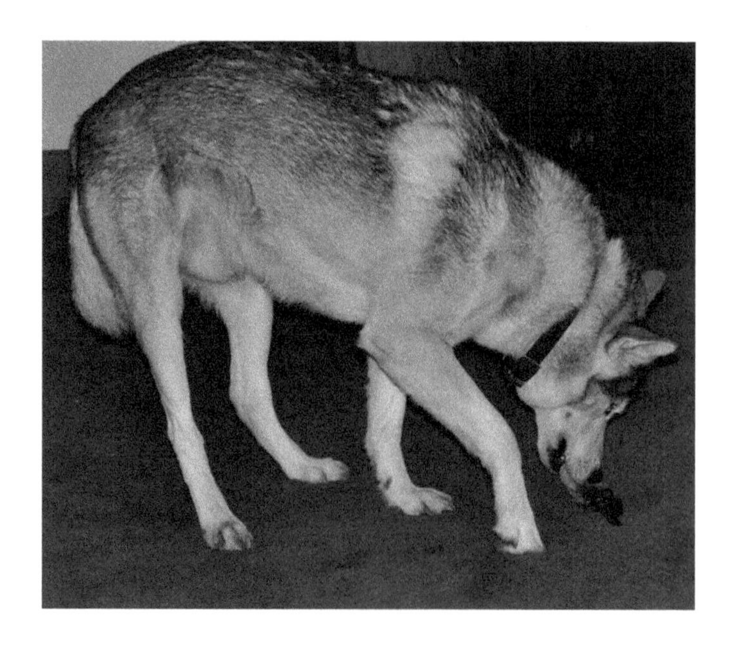

Hearing three special words, "I can't finish,"
here he comes to save the day!

Thanks, Hunter, now Mom won't be mad!

Anybody want to buy a brown truck?

HC 26: THE DIFFERENCE BETWEEN A DISASTER AND AN INCONVENIENCE IS PREPARATION

Texas—cowboys, oil, and unpredictable weather. Well, the attributes of Texas are so many that it will take a nuclear war to get me to leave—and maybe I'd rather die here than leave. But the territory has a downside, as does all "territories." Tornadoes are a rough thing to deal with, both mentally and physically. The truth is that when I first moved to the ranch, my weather-alert radio squawked and warned me of an approaching tornado, so I grabbed my 3 billion watt surplus flashlight to see firsthand what the funnel looked like. I stood for twenty minutes on the front porch, scanning the night sky for a funnel. *Nothing!* Stupid radio. The winds died down and I went to sleep.

The next morning I was a little bummed that I hadn't "seen" my tornado, but work beaconed, so I opened the front door and walked to the left stairs of the deck. Whoa! A four by four and 160 pounds of cement attached was lying by the stairs of the deck. It had come from a storage shed I built about six hundred yards away. It landed ten feet from where I was standing. Saying that the tornado hadn't shown up, wrong again.

"A man has to know his limitations," said Clint in *Magnum Force*. Wow! Did that hit home? I ordered a tornado shelter the next day. I've used it three times, and this is the story of one of those times.

The weather radio sounded and alerted my close friend Riki and me that a tornado was in Caddo Mills (twenty miles away) and heading east. It would hit Commerce in twenty minutes. Wow! Riki was cleaning his .45 (we had been shooting all afternoon). Twenty minutes. "Hey, I can be finished by then," he exclaimed. Hmmm.

Twenty minutes sounds like a long time. Twenty minutes till it hits Commerce, Texas. Hmmm.

I looked outside and the sky was a funny color. I ran to the "pen/suite," and the boys (Hunter and Jagger) followed. It was the safe thing to do, and they would be safe—or not. God giving a blessing—or not.

I kissed them both and ran back inside as hail plummeted the ranch and me. "It's time!" Riki yelled, and we headed for the front door. The lights flickered and the door exploded. We were four miles west of Commerce, and that made the difference. The funnel was over us and we were both knocked to the ground, and then we crawled to the tornado shelter, holding on to the picket fence and each other. Blinded by the rain, debris, and hail, we opened the door of the shelter and fell inside. The wind and noise soon subsided. We exited the shelter, and Riki exclaimed, "No damage!" I looked around and said, "Where's the carport? My shutters? The deck furniture? The fence? Oh my God!"

The carport had been lifted up and over and hit the wolf pen then up and hit the power cables and landed nearby, oh, a hundred yards or so.

Hunter's hair was on the cracked opening on the solid wall of the pen. What had he experienced? I've never seen him shaken. But he must have been shaken. He slept on my bed for two nights.

We haven't had such a close call since, but when the weather alert sounds, Hunter looks to me in a strange and attentive way. "Don't wait. Let's go now." The next time he'll be in the tornado shelter with me.

The carport, relocated by God.

The wolf-pen wall hit by the flying carport!

Note the "wolf hairs" as Hunter must have looked out of the hole to see what was happening!

HC 27: HOW LONG IS LONG ENOUGH?

When we fall in love, we set up a bad event. We think it's all bliss, love, and kisses, but there's going to be that moment. We will break up, or worse, one of us will die.

When we form a "couple," we are destined to suffer a loss. When a mother gives birth, she hopes her life will conclude in the proper order by dying before her son or daughter. It's okay because that is the order of things. When you lose a parent, you've lost your past. Your spouse? You've lost your present. And your child? Well, then you've lost your future. It's the worst, and I've seen the pain of that etched in a couple women in my life and couldn't do enough or anything for them. No one can.

I have always hated the pain of losing a pet, so I opted for having border collies as pets. They live from thirteen to twenty years. That means fewer "moments of pain." Yes, I'm a math freak. Those "events" are farther apart.

Buffy, my first border collie, was twenty years and four months old when she died. I was devastated and cried for days. A great friend (Mick Patton) purchased Jagger for me to "fill the gap." He wasn't Buffy. He was Jagger and I loved him so much. The first night I put him to bed, I said, "Good night, my prince." He was four years old when I acquired Hunter. Hunter always loved him as a mentor, teacher of toys, and brother, then playmate and respected elder. We all posed for pictures together, played, walked, watched TV, and just cuddled together. We were as much family or pack as any group could be.

I took pictures of us all together watching TV one night. I really don't know why, but it was the "Hold it in the left hand and try to look natural" type of photos. Later, when cell phones had cameras on board, they were dubbed "selfies."

The next morning, Jagger, now age fourteen, had thrown up in four places. He was shaking, and I laid down beside him to see if he was okay. His eyes shook violently from side to side. I looked at Hunter, and he walked to the pen as if to say, "Take him somewhere, someplace where they can make him better."

I carried Jagger to the car and raced to the vet. He said, "Where do we draw the line? He looks like he's had a severe stroke." He knows me and I answered as expected. "Do everything. He's my little boy"

He took my boy and I returned to a confused Hunter. That evening I walked into the guest room and thought Hunter was also sick. No, he had left a pile of food in the guest room. Weird? Then as I was turning off the lights for the night, I noticed a pile in my office, living room, my bedroom, and in my closet. Oh my God, he was hoping that if Jagger came back, he would have a snack, no matter where here ended up.

That was Saturday night. Monday I was at the vet at 8:00 a.m. when they opened. Jagger was worse and had shown no brain function. Gary, the vet, and I walked to the back, and I had the last sacred moments with my loyal friend, his last breath filling my tear-filled face. The words came out for the last time. "Good night, my prince." For the next three nights, Hunter sat all night on the back deck and howled long and haunting howls. A wolf howls to let you know where he is and/or the way home. I cried; he howled. After three nights he stopped, and I wouldn't know why for five weeks.

These are the pictures taken the night before Jagger's stroke.

Jagger trying to make me laugh. Jagger, my little Prince.

HC 28: A PACK NEEDS TO BE A PACK

When Jagger died, Hunter was devastated. He seemed to say, "The pain is too much. I miss him. I need a pack.

Becky called me on the day I left, and she was in a panic. Hunter was howling and he needed a pal. She would bring over a friend's dog, but I better "fill up the pack."

I called the Rockwall humane society, and a nice lady said they had a male border collie. I said I'd be there at five thirty. It was Friday and they closed at 6:00 p.m. I asked if I could put a credit card hold on him, and she said no. It was 3:48 p.m. I had it made. Then three accidents and very slow traffic. Stopped traffic and my ETA on the GPS was 6:10 p.m. I called and asked the young man who answered, "Could you hang around past six o'clock?"

"Why?" he questioned.

"I'm running late, and I want the border collie."

"We don't have a border collie." I felt like I was in *The Twilight Zone*. The girl had called a prospect and said that if she wanted the border, she'd better get there quick. Really nice.

I was crushed and mentioned it to my vet who was cremating Jagger. He said the Commerce Animal Shelter had a border. I called and they were gone for the weekend. I left a message that I'd be there at 9:00 a.m. Monday. Then a friend said that Quinlan had a rescue Shelter, open on Saturday. That's where I met Harrison.

Hunter was so happy, but I had given my word to the Commerce Animal Shlter, and so I went Monday to tell them I already had a dog. That's where I met Dottie.

So I "rescued" Dottie and Harrison.

Dottie couldn't come home for a couple days. I had her spade and felt a little recovery time would be good before meeting the man of her dreams. Harrison was home right away.

Hunter liked Dottie right off, maybe because he had never spent a lot of time around a female, and it was very interesting for him. He couldn't seem to understand the perpetual energy of a puppy. He was never like that, so it seemed to irritate him.

Little Harrison would steal a squeaky toy and run. Running was useless. He would run a hundred steps, and Hunter was there in one jump. Hunter didn't get mad because he always caught Harrison and retrieved the toy. Soon Harrison learned to hide them for "another day." It was all very funny to watch.

For Hunter's sanity, I kept the little one in the laundry room or in the backyard most of the time. Dottie would play with Harrison then play with Hunter. Over the next five months, the group time increased, and calmness entered the pack. Hunter and I scheduled a lot of alone time, which he seems to cherish. Often after dinner I'll put Harrison and Dottie in the backyard, and Hunter and I will walk the ranch. Last night was a great one. A full moon so no night vision was necessary. Hunter and I walked for nearly an hour, smelling and recording the position of everything! Then we spent a few minutes on the front porch, watching the stars. A beautiful November Texas night. After almost an hour of "group time," Hunter was tired of the energy level of Harri. Yes, he's only Harrison when he's being reprimanded.

Brave Harri steals a squeaky toy.

Hunter and Dottie were an instant couple!

Hunter was fascinated with Harri, but Harri was a little shaken at the size of his new friend.

Harri's first bone was a highlight of his weekend.

Big weekend, big wolf, big sleep

HC 29: A PET PSYCHIC? YOU HAVE GOT TO BE KIDDING!

There's a day that you have to "take charge." You have to "man up." My dearest neighbors are not rich. Actually, they think I am, and I'm not. But life is relative and so yes.

Anyway, Becky is a loving woman who adores her horses, her dogs, and their babies. So when she told me that she had had a "pet psychic" out to "talk" to her mare about the recent trampling of her colt and how she felt about it, how it would affect her life, *okay*. At $150 an hour, I was angry! I wanted to get this "psychic" and rip her lungs out. How dare she take advantage of a couple who just—well, they make ends meet because I pay for them to house sit when I'm traveling on the road. I love them like family and it works, but not with the financial drain of a psychic. I asked Becky to get the "psychic" to come out and "talk" to Hunter. I was setting a trap. I would expose the psychic and get Becky's money back!

Sandra showed up around 12:15 p.m. I was insistent that Becky be there for the "communication." I couldn't wait.

She met Hunter and fell in love as so many had. I wasn't impressed. "He loves you so much. He says you're the best human in the world. He feels so equal and happy with you. You are his fellow traveler in the spirit world."

Really! Hello? Tell me something! Actually, tell me something I don't *want to hear*!

"How old was he when you got him?"

"Five weeks. Why?"

She wrinkled her face. "That's odd, because he doesn't remember his parents. At five weeks he should."

"He was taken out of the wolf pen at the zoo because of an ice storm at two weeks and fed goat's milk." She smiled at she pet Hunter. "That would explain it."

Weird.

That was it. I was ready. This lady was through. "What's Hunter's favorite thing?" She doesn't say beef ribs cooked at 350 degrees for forty-five minutes, cooled for forty-five minutes, and—*oh yeah!* She's going to be thrown out on her ear. No more wishy-washy "What's Hunter's favorite thing?"

She looked perplexed. Why? "This is funny. When I drove up, I didn't see a pickup"

"What?" I said. No beef ribs? "My pickup is in the shop. Why?"

"Oh, that explains it. He says that he loves it when you wear the night vision and drive him out to see the horses and donkeys." Well, you can think and say and fill in what you want. I was stone-cold shocked. You know, *jaw on the floor.*

Nobody knew about the night vision, and nobody knew about the trips to the back fields.

And the next fifty answers were just as shocking. "What was the funniest moment you remember, Hunter?"

"He says you were walking him, you were wearing night vision, on a leash, and Jagger, who couldn't see as well, was running wildly in circles. Then Jagger ran into a pond. He had to sit down. Too funny. He says he misses Jagger." Then she looked at Hunter and said, "Hasn't he visited you?" Hunter jumped up as if he been zapped! "Because I talk to animals, and I know that after a few days, they can visit you." Hunter relaxed and snuggled up to her again. Okay, folks, I may be a dumb guy, but this was too much, too real, too unknown. She *was* the real thing. She told me what Hunter thought and told him what he already knew. I love him and always will. We actually got to "talk." I'll never be the same. What started out to be a moment of truth, the exposing of a charlatan, ended up as a tear-filled communication of the surrogate alpha and the beta wolf, friends and family forever. By the way, if you haven't figured it out, I love my wolf.

And now look at his face when I kiss his head.

A family member being "set straight"!

Soon all is "forgive and forget." *But learn!*

HC 30: HEROES? YOU NEVER CHOOSE TO BE ONE, BUT ONE DAY YOU ARE ONE

I grew up in a great time and place in history. At eleven years old, I watched JFK give his inaugural speech. Add to that the astronauts, Chuck Yeager, the Beatles, Stones, and Beach boys. Roger Maris and Micky Mantle. Ali, Frazier, and Foreman. Newman, Brando, and McQueen. In those days, the world was filled with heroes. Now? Good luck, and most of those "would-be" heroes would say, "I never asked to be a hero."

No one does. No one has a choice. Right now, stop reading and think for a second about those who look up to you. You are a hero too, plan it or not, like it or not.

Hunter's impression of Harrison was getting more tainted every day. At first he was so happy to see a baby, a border collie like the dearly missed Jagger. But Jagger was mature and fun. He played, then slept, then ate and relaxed, watched TV, and chewed his tennis ball. At bedtime he would sleep on the floor next to me or hop up and lay next to me on the bed, his head facing Hunter and away from me. Hunter, I think, expected Harrison to be a small version of Jagger, relaxed and at peace with the world, reserved and observant like Hunter when he was a young one. Harri was a puppy, excited about the chair, the wall, the door, the inside and outside. He went nuts over dry food—twice a day! And he couldn't stop wanting to jump on Hunter.

Hunter, for the first time in his life, would curl his lips and snarl at Harri. Harry didn't get used to it. He just started running up to Hunter and sliding as if into second base, slide with his underbelly exposed, and kiss the air until Hunter's face got close. Then he kissed as many times as he could until he got "snarled at."

The scene was repeated too many times every day. Hunter was sure Harri would stop this soon and "man up." Harri was sure he could win over Hunter with his puppy breath and good looks. I've maneuvered the two, as has Becky, the house sitter, so that they spend time together and time apart. Dottie's heartworm test came back positive, so she had to take some severe meds and stay calm. Not here! So she had a thirty-day "spa stay" at the vet's, tranquilized, and relaxed to get rid of the debris of the dead worms. That left the boys alone, up close, and personal—for thirty days. After twenty days, they had come to the agreement of "Don't ask, don't tell." Harri couldn't stop watching Hunter, and Hunter didn't want to know why.

It was the first of the "cooler than normal" nights this fall, and when Hunter opened the sliding glass door to the back deck, I relaxed. The cool, crisp evening air was welcome and would add to a great night's sleep. I do recall a noise. A stumble? And fall down the stairs? I soon heard Hunter enter, kiss me, and hop into bed. A long sigh and he was asleep for the night, and so was I.

The next morning was a early one. I needed to be in Paris at 9:00 a.m., so everyone had to chop-chop! Get going.

I walked outside and Hunter looked at me. "We got to go to work." That phrase meant "Get in the pen." He trotted across the deck, looked to his left, then continued toward the pen.

At the left of the stairs was a dead possum, his throat removed. I said *"Hunter!"* and he turned as if something was wrong, so I praised him. "You protected us. You guarded us from the possum. What a good wolf." He was happy and finished the walk to the pen. As I turned, I saw Harri standing up and watching the whole event. What did he think?

When I returned from my scheduled appointment, I went to the back deck and Harry was acting crazy. He was needing some attention. Oh my God, he had captured and killed a frog and left him on the back deck. Am I nuts? No, Hunter was a hero. Harri knew it and wanted to be one too.

Dottie and Harri Play in the water hose.

Hunter and Harri get the first kisses in. Hunter is a hero.

Ted, a close friend, plays with the new kids.

HC 31: ANYONE WANT TO REDECORATE?

Becky, Hunter's house sitter, and I have an agreement. It's more of an attitude, something that makes life easier to endure the "edgy" moments. Simply, it is a sentence that as you say the words in time of crisis, makes it all easier to handle.

"If that's the worst thing that happens today, it'll be a great day."

Try it. You'll like it. Well, on this occasion, it wasn't enough to help Becky. Harri loved to get under the house then out the front picket fence and run the ranch. I figured that as he got bigger, one day he wouldn't be able to slip through the small openings in the deck skirt, and it would end.

Well, instead he learned how to pull off the next board, making a larger hole and he was off to adventure. I replaced a few boards, and in a day or two, he'd find some older loose boards and off again, always returning when I called him and proud to show off his skills. Rather than Harrison, maybe I should have named him Houdini!

Now, you may think that this is a misprint, but read it carefully. You can't make this up. Harri, tired of being confined to a 75' × 130' playground, decided to tunnel out under the fence. Hunter sees this event and tunnels out after him—correct, not to escape but to retrieve and return Harri! A wolf goes out to retrieve a border collie! He chases him and corners him time and time again and finally chases him back through the tunnel. I warned you to read this slowly. Well, Becky was amused, but still she knows that her main duty is to protect Hunter from everything, including himself.

At night she usually stays in the guest room and lets the kids have the run of the roost. With Hunter, that means indoors and out. As you know, he's a sliding-door expert. She figures (rightly so) that the combo of a doorman and a fence man isn't in anyone's best interest. So she puts Harri in the backyard, with Dottie and Hunter in the house with the sliding door *locked.* This was a safe move for the night, and I would be home in the morning. At 5:15 a.m. she woke to hear Hunter's whining at her door. Figuring he couldn't "hold it" any longer, she opened the door and walked to the living area.

Her heart stopped as she turned on the lights and saw that Hunter had redecorated the window dressings. Harri would have made noises outside, and Hunter couldn't stand not knowing, not seeing what was going on. She mustered up courage and called me on my cell. No answer because I left it in my car that night. In a robotic state of shock, she vacuumed the wood-blind splinters and wondered how I would react to her "judgment call." Later she put Dottie and Hunter in their La Quinta Lobo Suite and went home to feed her horses and fret (not necessarily in that order). Well, at that time, I went to the car to get my phone and eat breakfast in the hotel lobby. When I saw a missed call at 5:24 a.m. from my house, I panicked. I knew by the normal procedure that (1) Hunter was dead, had run away, etc.; (2) the house burnt down; (3) some unthinkable event. My message retrieval didn't work. I dialed my house, no answer. I dialed Becky's house (she was out feeding horses), no answer. OMG! Her husband must be dead too. She would be at the morgue, identifying the bodies of Hunter and her husband. Poor thing. Where would she stay with both houses burned to the ground? I was sure I had it all figured out when the phone rang. Blinds? I burst out laughing. Our houses were safe. Hunter and Don were alive. Blinds? If that's the worst thing that happens today, it's going to be a great day.

Wasn't Houdini's name Harry?

Hunter and Dottie waiting for my return.

Hunter's redecorating! More light for sure.

HC 32: HUNTER AND DIRTY HARRI

With all the new family members and winter 'round the bend, a trip to Petsmart to buy a doggie door was in order. I was sure that the two border collies would figure out the door in no time, but I was worried about the opening. I wasn't sure if Hunter could fit through it. It was labeled *big dog* not *big wolf*! I didn't measure or even hesitate buying the door, because Hunter always found a way with doors. In the suburbs of Dallas, we had a master-bedroom door that was a stick handle. He'd just paw it down and push. Hunter always figured it out. This door also had a "slide in" blocker to "keep them out" or in when you needed. Easy to install and soon the big test. Was Hunter too big?

Hunter caught on in a flash and fit with the ducking of his shoulders. The next day Harri did too, but Dottie was mystified by the moving flap and noise. Harri began a procession of taking "stuff" out the door flap and loved his new freedom. Every now and then, getting "stuff" caught in the door. Harri was baffled as to why my king-size bed pillow wouldn't get through the doggy door.

On New Year's Day I planned a barbecue, inviting only my closest local friends, people I trusted with Hunter and my life. Hunter was usually confined to his "wolf suite" during larger gatherings because I wasn't sure of everyone's ability to watch the front doors. With this group he just walked around and said hi in his very personal way. As I have said before, Hunter acts differently toward everyone, and the party was eye candy to me. He gave the high five to Brad then rubbed up against Briley, stood, and kissed Alan. What a character. He made the rounds many times that night and always greeted with his individual "wolf ways." Most everyone gave Hunter a snack, and he acted like they were the only person who cared about his hunger problems. Poor starving boy hadn't had ribs in over twenty hours! At the end of the night, a few friends sang karaoke and we all laughed, sang, and slowly dispersed, Hunter kissing everyone goodbye. I couldn't help but smile as the last guest left and I hit the pillow. Hunter hopped up on his bed, Dottie snuggled next to me, and Harri—well, Harri just stood there as if to say, "Sleep? I'm just getting going!" Reluctantly he faded off to sleep in a few moments. The next day, a lady came by from the battered-women's clinic and resale shop to pick up some clothing donations. She was amazed at Hunter, and Hunter was at his most amazing. I closed the block lock on the doggy door so Harri and Hunter wouldn't run in and out. Hunter amazed me by getting right through it! I gave her the clothes and walked her to the gate. When I returned, I looked at my night table. My carry pistol was missing. I called the cell she'd called me from earlier. "Oh no, there wasn't a gun between the T-shirts." How did she know so quickly? I thought the worst. I last saw it before the New Year's Day get-together, but I trusted the attendees with my life, every one of them. I emptied every one of my bedroom drawers and had no sleep for a couple days. I did the police reports, etc. I looked everywhere, including the backyard "just in case." Then it snowed, a rarity for East Texas, and as I looked up from my computer, I grabbed my camera and began laughing from relief and the humor of the moment. I opened the door and yelled, "Harri! Put the gun down and step away. Paws on the ground." The pictures are real. Everyone loved the story, and the police requested some photos. I guess for Harri's file. I've taken appropriate steps. Renamed him. Dirty Harri!

HC 33: THE GREAT ESCAPES AS IN MANY

The skirting on my home was now entering it's ninth year. I think it was treated lumber, but thirty-six seasons is a lot—heat, wet, cold, rain, and wind. In the early days at the ranch, Hunter would just leap over the fence, but after I installed hot wires, that came to an abrupt halt. Two years later, I turned off the fence but Hunter never tried again. Just the sight of the wires reminded him of that "shocking" event. Hunter was never a digger, but Harri was and Dottie was getting more mischievous every day. Harri was digging near the skirting, and Dottie just decided that the old boards may look like a barrier but the temptation was too great not to "try" them. After all, what's the sense of living on a hundred-acre ranch if you have to wait for Dad to get the leashes out before you can go for a walk.

I was working on reports in the living room when the silence became overwhelming. I checked in the backyard and saw a two–plank-wide hole in the skirting. I went out front, hopped on the ATV, and searched for about an hour. No sign of the convicts. I returned to my reports, hoping this would end as they usually did—Hunter coming home and chasing donkeys till he tires then going for a swim to cool his feet, and then I'd get him as he walked from the pond. It had been three hours, so I saved my worked and walked to the front door. There on the deck stood the three musketeers!

I guess they were happy and the field trip had ended. They all trotted by me then through to my bedroom door and into the backyard then to their pen and into it!

I locked the door and smiled as I repaired the skirting. Checking a few other boards that had rotted bottoms, I spent the afternoon replacing the weak ones.

Once Hunter had seen Dottie create a hole, he began prying the boards off almost at will. They would head out and return a few hours later. No harm, no foul. Well, not exactly. I was harmed. I was worried sick from the minute he left until he returned. The fear and reality of someone shooting Hunter was numbing.

On a hot day in August of 2011, Hunter, Dottie, and Harri made the usual escape, this time digging under the fence—a new tactic in the war games. The fence boards had snapped off during the digging process, helping the project along considerably. My third look out the front door produced a gasp. There on the deck were Harri and Dottie, no Hunter. I quickly whisked them off to the pen and I repaired the fence. Where was Hunter?

I got on the ATV and did the rounds of the land. About thirty-five acres are wooded with several creeks and four ponds. Oh yes, a lot of hiding places, but Hunter had never hidden, he was a runner. A wolf can cover a huge distance in a short amount of time, so why didn't he come home? Was he hurt, shot, or trapped?

I was heading back to the ranch house in hopes that he had returned when I saw several donkeys racing out of a creek bed. Close behind was my boy, tongue hanging *way, way* out. I followed him for about twenty more minutes when he just stopped running (chasing really) and looked at me, exhausted. I walked over, and he actually raised his head to allow me to clamp his leash on his collar. We walked to the nearby pond and he cooled down. I got some amazing photographs of him in the pond and we had a great walk back.

Success breeds excitement, and the war of the skirt and fences continued on a regular basis. I repair, they figure out a new twist on the game. They always return, but it's that nagging fear I have. I can't control it, and Hunter doesn't understand it; he's a wolf and he is invincible! After Dottie was at my sister's house for a few months, Thanksgiving rolled around. Dottie sat at my feet or next to me on the couch every minute I was there. It got to me and I took her home that night. Right away she began biting Hunter and yelling at him with that "wife bark." Carol took her back the next day and was shocked to see "that" side of Dottie when she was around Hunter. Weird. The escape last month involved Harri and Hunter, Hunter chasing three donkeys and me on the ATV right next to him, Harri running about a hundred feet behind us. He was sure he was needed back there doing something. We finally herded the donkeys into the front field, and the horses decided that they'd seen enough and chased Hunter into the front pond. Hunter looked to me for help, and I rode the ATV to the crest of the pond, between the horses and Hunter. Yelling at the horse with animated arms must have looked crazy, but they ran off bucking and snorting, and Hunter waded out next to me. We watched them leave and we walked back to the house. Harri continued to lag behind, maybe out of fear of everyone being bigger than him!

Last week's run may have been the last for a while. Hunter opened up the last of the unreinforced skirt boards, and he and Harri started yet another adventure. After an hour I stood on the front deck and saw them about two hundred yards away. I whistled for them and Harri turned to look at me. He raced home with Hunter close behind. They ran through where they escaped and trotted into the pen. After a hearty laugh and the skirt repair and reinforcement, I laid a hot wire around the bottom of the fence. When I let them out, Hunter just stared at it and walked inside. Not Happy. Ribs and a game of squeaky toy changed that.

HC 34: I THOUGHT IT WAS AGE

Hunter was getting lethargic, sleeping even more and playing less, less wrestling and more snuggling. He had had two bumps on his back, but everyone said that was normal for northern K9 in a hot climate like Texas. I, of course, was worried and felt very little reassurance by these opinions.

Then my house sitter said something that would change everything. When I mentioned his near constant panting, she said, "Well, he's got two huge hemorrhoids hanging out of his butt!" Not being a butt watcher myself (at least with animals), I hadn't noticed but now I was very concerned. The next morning I took Hunter to the vet, and when the girl asked what was wrong, I simply asked, "Do wolves get hemorrhoids?" She smiled and said, "No."

"Then we have a problem," I moaned.

Gary Thompson is a friendly and brilliant vet and (most importantly, he loves Hunter).

After a complete exam and blood samples, he sent me home with some pills to ease any pain and kill any infections. Two days later he recommended Hunter have an operation, have the tumors removed and biopsied. Was I scared? You bet.

I often wake up in the many hotels and can smell Hunter's coat. It's not unlike a man or woman missing their spouse and imagining the scent of cologne or perfume. I miss him all the time we're apart. When I'm gone he, suffers separation anxiety on the fourth night, so I limit most trips to three nights or less. Okay, I get it too. We have an amazing bond. I prayed for the best possible outcome.

I had to show off new products Thursday; the vet would be out of town Friday, so the staff met me at 7:30 a.m. to take Hunter on Thursday morning! When Gary called after the operation, I was elated. Hunter was out okay, awake, and in relatively little pain. Gary said that the lumps on his back were pretty easy to deal with, but the others hereafter known as "others" looked very bad, and they were deeply inset. Hunter would be best to stay there till Saturday morning, and the biopsy results would take a week. A week. Jeez! I'm a worrier; that's a year in worrier time.

Picking Hunter up Saturday was a hoot. He was given the famous "cone of shame," and the camera had to come out. He couldn't get through the doggy door, and the photo of his face in that cone—priceless! I stocked up on smoked Sausage to hide the meds in, and the balance of the week showed an increasingly energetic Hunter. Then the call came from Gary about the biopsy results. I could see my watch slowing down as his words became lower in pitch and very elongated. I wanted to hear the complete sentence, but it seemed to be growing in length. Then the word, my new favorite word—"benign." I felt all my fears leave! It was as if I had heard "B-9" and I was the big bingo winner!

Hugs and kisses were even more special than usual that night. Hunter's recovery over the next few weeks was amazing, and the playing and pranks that were Hunter's special nature returned to my life with my best friend and partner. Even with the "cone of shame," he leaped when I came home! If you have your health, you have everything.

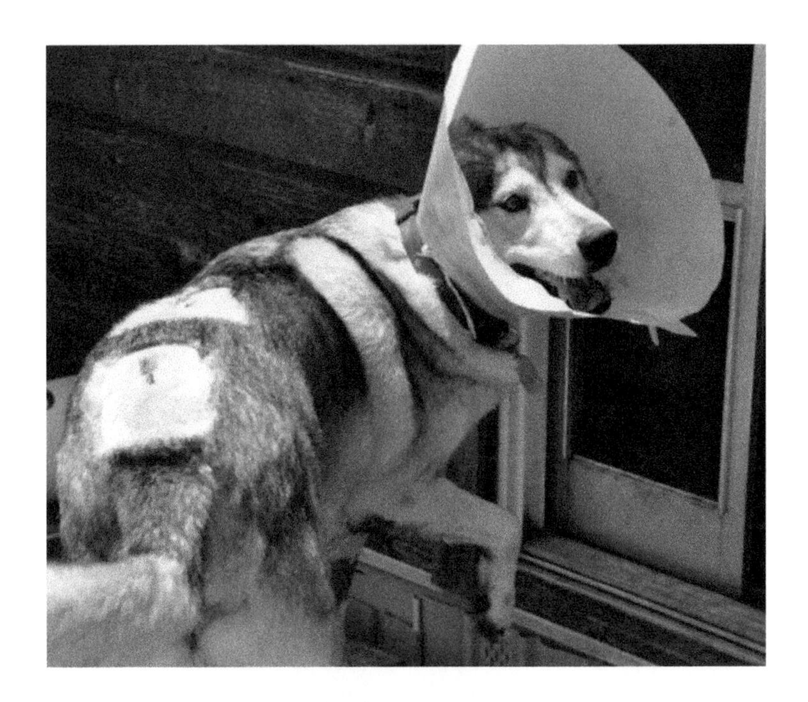

HC 35: THE SWIMMERS—EVERYONE HAS TO COOL OFF!

It was a day of writing. My job has boiled down to training and writing articles for the music market. Anyway, several days a month, I just sit at my home computer and create these articles. Hunter and Harri usually come and go, but mostly they sit on the couch next to me or on the floor by my feet. So when it's really quiet and I can't see them, it's most likely another "They got bored," "They pulled a skirting board off the house," "They ran under the house," "The boys are out exploring the ranch," in that order. I refer to it as an escape.

For the ten years I've been out here, I got totally freaked and worried every time they "escaped" because I was sure some redneck would see Hunter and shoot him. Then I would find the guy and beat him to death and you know all that paperwork! But this time I was cool. I found the hole and realized the boys were gone. I calmly walked inside, took a shower, and got dressed to get them. Oh yeah, I'll take my camera just in case a photo op pops up!

I walked outside and saw the donkeys running out of the woods. Ahhh! Not ten minutes later, Hunter and Harri came out of the woods. Now Hunter always cools his feet off in a pond, and this time of year, all but one is mostly dried up. Not the big pond, that one is fourteen feet deep! That's where they would head, and I'd be ready. But as I rode over to the pond, they both just ran up to me and stood by the ATV. I grabbed Hunter's collar and slipped the leash on. Then I looked at the two boys. What harm had they done? It was a hot day, and we were right by the pond. A cool swim was just thirty-five feet away. I undid the snap on Hunter's collar, pointed to the pond, and yelled you guys are hot. Go cool off. They ran together and jumped in. Harri was a bit nervous and sat in the shallow end, but Hunter went for a swim. Actually, he did laps of the pond. I guess he watched the Olympics with me and learned to go back and forth. I hoped he didn't want a medal!

They kept swimming for about twenty to twenty-five minutes and I snapped away. Harri was a couple years old now, and Hunter had accepted him as a friend, and as friends they played. It was a good day. An adventure in the woods and back fields chasing the donkeys then a swim in the pond. They then came out and I put the leash on Hunter, and we all walked back to the house and they watched as I fixed the new hole in the wall. That night it was a beef-ribs dinner and a solid sleep. I guess it's pretty exhausting chasing those big guys then competing in the four-hundred-yard swim. I know I was smiling remembering all those photographs. Oh yeah, and I was thinking what a great chronicle this day would make.

HC 36: A GENTLE HUNTER WOLFS IT DOWN!

"Look at him wolf that down!" How many times did I hear that as a child? Then after acquiring Hunter, I was enlightened to the fact that as a wolf he was very gentle with his food, often eating omelets from a fork. Weird but true. The only time he really got crazy was when I would shoot a screaming monkey through the air. If you haven't seen one, they are very funny as they fly (their arms are rubber bands to launch them). They scream this amazing monkey call. Well, Hunter just went nuts the first time I brought one home. Then, when he realized that he could make them scream by shaking them, well, his world was never the same. I buy them by the dozen, and he knows what drawer I keep them in. If I get near that drawer, he's there and ready! Snack time is actually funny because little Harri snaps at everything—a sausage, a meatball, a shadow, anything—and Hunter just waits, and when he's fed, he takes the treat and chews it!

Well, all that changed one day, the day before Christmas. Maybe it's the fact that Hunter's birthday is December 25. Yeah, he's a Christmas baby and the best gift anyone could ever ask for. For the record, he was twelve this Christmas. Maybe it was the delivery girl. Victoria is a young photographer/model who has taken hundreds of photos of and with Hunter. The day before Christmas, as my nephew and I were fixing a fence, she showed up with Hunter and Harri's Christmas gifts. She had purchased a bone for Hunter and figured that he and Harri might like some dog treats. She told me the story, and we both thought the "funny" part was in the store. She had gone to Commerce's only pet store and asked the clerk if she had any treats for her friend's pet. "He has a wolf." The clerk responded, "Yes, we have some *woof sticks*." Victoria thought the clerk said *wolf sticks*, and so she was amazed! When she saw the label, she started laughing at the error and muttered "Woof woof woof." Where was the *L*? Woof woof.

The best was yet to come. She handed Hunter the bone and he walked around with it, then she opened the bag of "woof sticks." Hunter dropped the bone; Harri grabbed the bone and ran. You would too. Hunter fixed a stare at Victoria. So intent was this look that Harri dropped the bone twenty feet away and returned to see what could be so interesting. She handed Hunter the treat, and my nephew Tim grabbed his camera. Good thing because no one who knows Hunter would believe it. He ate the treat, and as she tossed one to Harri, Hunter leaped up (Victoria is about five foot ten) and kissed her face so hard, she nearly fell over backward! The frenzy was on, and we were amazed and amused to see my gentle giant gone berserk. Hunter circled and jumped and howled for more, and when they were all gone, Victoria held the empty bag high in the air. Hunter jumped higher than I've ever seen and jammed his face into the bag! Now Hunter can easily clear an eight-foot fence, so he was coming up as he hit the bag, ripping it from Victoria's hand. The pictures are the proof, and I can't wait to buy these by the carton. The three of us had a great laugh, and Hunter got a fantastic treat for his twelfth birthday.

Victoria left, and Tim and I reviewed the photographs. Yep, Hunter went crazy for these treats and wolfed them down!

HC 37: THE RITUALS

On the mornings that I wake up before Hunter, I often just watch him. He's so beautiful that this is a great pleasure. His majestic giant frame cuddled on the bed he's slept on since he was six months old. The pillow he rests his head on is labeled in camo letters "Hunter." It's such a beautiful picture that though I have many, I have to grab my camera/phone and snap one more of my sweetheart of a friend. His eyes blink then he focuses and turns first to my bed, making sure I'm still there. A little wag of the tail as he sees me looking back at him and I say, "Morning, Hunter." Then of course, Harri wiggles and I extend a hand to his head. Harri sleeps on the pillow next to me. "Morning, Harri." After Hunter observes the status of everything in the room, he will get off his bed with a grunt and a wag. Then sitting very still and in perfect posture, he leans deeply in each direction. Forward, backward, left, then right. It's morning wolf yoga and it's so cool. He then hops up on my bed, and Harri wiggles over to kiss him. Hunter kisses me and looks around. It's as if he's summing up the wonders and treasures of his life. Slowly wagging his tail, he stares at me and often speaks that crazy wolf warble then hops to the floor. He and Harri go outside and do their morning rituals and return within a minute or two. Hunter, a big guy, often bumps his back on the huge doggy door. Once, just before he had the bumps (tumors) removed, I heard that bumping noise and felt a sharp searing pain in my back. Oh! No, please, no back pain today, but it subsided almost immediately. Hunter and Harri came wagging to my side of the bed. Very typical, but that morning there was blood on Hunter's back. He had ripped the "bump" from his back. Hmmm. Is that what I had felt? Exactly the same moment as he tore it off, I had that searing pain. Yes, over these twelve years, we had indeed become *that* close! What a blessing to become a kindred spirit of my best friend, a wolf—Hunter.

Sundays and Holidays are different. How does he know? Every Sunday and Holiday, Christmas, New Year's Day, Thanksgiving. He hops on my bed and buries his head in the sheets, his giant nose burrowing under me. He rolls over for belly rubs and extends his hand for a "high-five." We three wrestle and play for about an hour. It's a day of rest and fun, and somehow he knows it!

I send these Chronicles to Shirley at the *Tannehill Trader* as well as share them with my friends. I receive many notes and e-mails about them back from everyone. Many of my friends and acquaintances have come to the ranch to meet and greet with Hunter, and it's always his pleasure to meet new and old friends. He's just remarkable at remembering people. *He* will establish a way with each person and *always* greet that person with their special nods and wagging and kisses. Man, does he love women! When a wonderful lady visited for the first time, he summed up the situation and judged her instantly to be a wonderful person, running to her he gave her flying kisses! Yes, that is exactly what you think. He jumps up on her or even jumps by her and extends his head out licking her face! She looked at me and asked, "Does he react to everyone like this?" I couldn't resist as he had begun his annual shedding, and she was instantly covered in wolf hair. "Only those who wear black!"

So if you ever get to get near my ranch and meet Hunter, don't wear black!

HC 38: I'M NURSING HUNTER

When Hunter had the Tumors removed from his back and rear, the vet gave me some advice. "These are all testosterone based. You never had Hunter 'fixed,' and I think you should. Even though he's twelve years old, it would be the best thing for his immediate health and his longevity." Well, I was so excited to get him home and have him playing with Harri and me that I just put all that out of my mind. It's been a year since that operation, and we've had a great year full of night walks, ribs, treats, and visitors. But not a day goes by that I don't wish he could live forever. Wolves are strange and unknown creatures, but one thing is a fact. They live longer when they are needed, and I need Hunter. I thought I was the only one but that wasn't true.

When I made his appointment, the girl handed me a card that had the reminder time, date, and OMG, a note! No food or water after 10:00 p.m. Monday night! Okay, so I set a reminder alarm on my cell for 9:00 p.m. I really have to think this out because Hunter is really smart! He's got water in the "wolf hotel," so that's got to be locked up. Then the doors to the backyard have to be secured because he can open them. Then his indoor water and food dispenser have to be put on top of the refrigerator. Anything else? *Yes!* All the toilets have to be taped shut! Hunter watched this whole ordeal with very suspicious eyes. Dad had gone nuts or something big was in the works.

About eleven thirty that night, a monster Texas thunderstorm arrived. The lightning strikes were very close, and soon the power went out. Harri, being a border collie, was shaking like a leaf, Hunter just excited by the light show.

At 2:12 a.m., Hunter is licking my face and howling with a great deal of urgency. Of course, he *has to go*! So I watch him intently as he does his stuff in the rain. He doesn't drink anything and runs back inside the lockdown.

The next morning he checks all three toilets to see if I made any mistakes during the night. A confused Harri watches me put a leash on Hunter and leave. The drop-off goes smooth, and they agree that they should keep Hunter for one night.

During my day in my home office, Harri is an emotional wreck. He has never had a day without Hunter at his side. At one point, exhausted from stress, he falls asleep with his paw on my foot. The storm knocked out my modem, and when the repairman arrived, the normally "in your face" Harri hid in the far bathroom. No courage without a wolf at his side.

At 5:00 p.m., a frantic call from the vet. Hunter had eaten his way out of the cage! I raced to the vet, and brought a very groggy (and cross-eyed) Hunter home to a very happy Harri. I slept beside Hunter on the floor that night as he whimpered through the night, Harri six inches away.

In the morning Hunter and Harri were looking pretty normal. That was good news because I had scheduled Harri for his annual check up at 8:00 a.m. The boys frolicked and headed for the "wolf hotel." That's when it happened. I put the leash on Harri, and Hunter started screaming, howling, and running around the pen. I walked out with Harri fighting every step of the way. What did Hunter think was about to happen to Harri? I'll never know, but he was grabbing the chain-link fence with his teeth as if to chew his way out and save Harri! I put Harri in the van and returned to the backyard to talk and calm Hunter down. After a few minutes, I drove to the vet, dropped Harri off, and raced home. Hunter whined and cried at me for twenty minutes. Later that afternoon, I picked up Harri and everyone is now back in sync, together, and happy. I think I'm even wagging my tail!

HC 39: THE MAGIC TOUCH

I was going to name this chronicle "Campfire Stories" because it covers several subjects, but the magic touch was too special.

Over the years, my friends have always thought about Hunter in the nicest ways. Regularly sending me "wolf things" from comforters to stick-on pictures of wolves, my friends have paid their respect to my big boy. It brings me a great deal of joy to know that his life is so well-known. I get squeaky toys pretty often from people. One of the best gifts was a fifty-piece supply of squeakers. Yep, squeakers to replace the ones that Hunter had destroyed in his toys. I didn't even know such a thing existed.

One night I was watching TV, and as usual, Hunter was lying on the couch beside me. That night he kept shifting his weight trying to get comfortable and just couldn't settle in. After a few minutes, he gave up and laid on the floor. Well, that position didn't suit him either, so he stood up, grabbed a pillow off the couch in his teeth, and tossed it on the floor! Then he lay down, and I guess that was what he needed because he let out a huge sigh and fell asleep. I just smiled and knew again that I was the luckiest guy in the world.

Each dinner treat is a special moment for Hunter. About two months ago, he began a new plan to tease Harri. He just sits with the beef rib or ham hock and waits till Harri is finished. After a few more minutes, he slowly chews his meal, driving Harri nuts that his is gone already! Now when it comes to pork ribs, they are gone so fast, it is hard to imagine he tastes anything. Lamb chops are my favorite, but they are a little pricy to feed the boys. However, I eat most of the meat off the bone then give them both a bone. This is really different. Once the two "ends" are finished, Harri gives the nucleus (really hard part) to Hunter, and with one loud snap, Hunter shatters the remaining piece. What a team they are. There is never any growling or fighting. It was like that with Jagger and now Harri. Really special living with these two.

That brings me to the magic touch. Ironically, that was the name of a rock band I played with for nine years during the sixties in Washington, DC. I never realized that at sixty-three, I would discover the real meaning of the name. Hunter reaches out and touches my leg when I walk by, gives me the high five in the mornings, and has on occasions wrapped his arms around the leg of someone he loves and howls. It's brought people to tears to realize that Hunter wants them to stay longer. I guess it's the feeling we get when holding hands. It deepens the bond of the moment and says "I love you" without words. Many times I have photographed Hunter's big paws on my foot, my leg, etc. Actually, he's really affectionate and loves that magic rouch. When I work in my home office, he will often sleep near Harri and extend his arm out to have that contact while he sleeps. Just like so many other of Hunter's rituals, Harri now does the same thing. I can't tell you how beautiful it is. I can't.

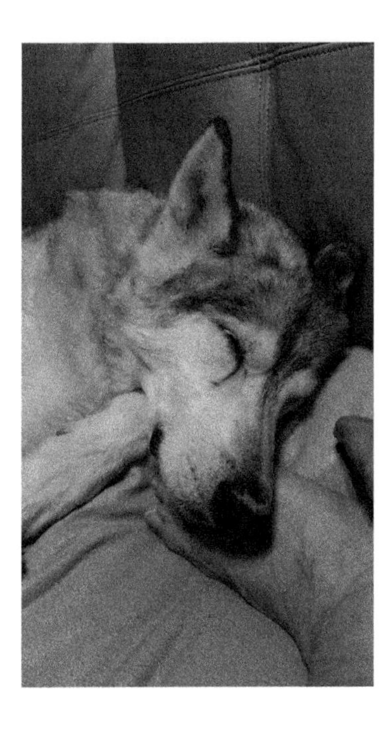

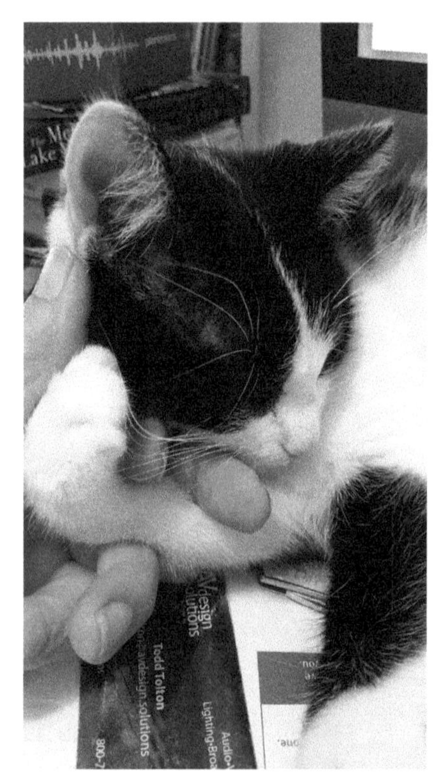
Todd Tolton

HC 40: WISER THAN I

At least once a week, I try to do something for myself, my sister, or both of us. This particular weekend it was a balloon festival in Celina, Texas. I didn't mind putting the boys in the "wolf suite" for the afternoon/evening because I had had a week of home-office days and we had shared some really close time.

Carol's family and I left around 4:00 p.m., and we're looking forward to seeing a great festival and taking some great photos. Once we arrived, we were surprised by a car show and carnival tied to the balloon fest! After lots of car photos, we wandered the carnival, and suddenly I looked over at Carol and knew I had to "come to the rescue." OMG, she had stopped at the animal section! Animals rescued, adoptions, etc., booths were all around her. She has four dogs and lives in suburbia, but she has a heart of gold. No platinum! Every other word that came from my mouth was *no*! She introduced me to all of the vendors as "My brother Rick owns a wolf." Pictures and stories of Hunter were told and retold. Come on, these are animal lovers, and they were captured by stories that seemed like fantasies in their world. One of the rescue sights gave me some "nature based" treats for Hunter, and Harri and I stuffed them in the bottom of my camera bag. The wind stirred up, and as the sun set, we left after witnessing several unsuccessful attempts at a balloon launch. We stopped for dinner at a "grass fed" burger place that was amazing. The day was great and fun but coming to a close. I dropped them off and headed home later than I had hoped for.

Hunter was howling the minute I came through the ranch gate as usual. It's hard not to smile when you live on a secluded hundred acres; the stars are bright and your wolf is happy to see you home with him again. A rack of beef ribs and then the long day was beginning to take its toll on me. Sleep came quickly.

I had left my camera bag at the front door, and so when I woke the next morning, I really was surprised when it was in my bedroom in the middle of the floor. Yes, my bag was there, and next to it was my 14–24 mm wide angle. What? What was all the other stuff? How did my camera bag get unzipped?

Well. Then I remembered the treats that the rescue people gave me! All the wrapping paper and packaging was strewn around the floor. Hunter had smelled the treats and unzipped the bag then found the treats under the lens and removed the lens and then the treats! I was again amazed by my big lug of a friend. He wasn't looking guilty or shy; as a matter of fact, he was lying near the camera bag in the midst of the clutter of wrapper debris, just content.

I guess I was the bad alpha for not handing out the food I had gathered the day before. He was better than I for forgiving me and finding the treats that I had forgotten. He was wiser than I and unzipped that pesky bag, gently removing the lens then getting what was rightfully his. Yes, he was a happy wolf and never even scolded me for my shortcomings and my short memory. The way he dealt with the situation proved he was wiser than I.

HC 41: HELL FREEZES OVER

I hate cats. They love you then leave you! So I will never have a cat!

It was a chilly but not really cold November 15, 2013, a couple days since the full moon, and the view was crystal. I took my camera and my biggest lens out to see what I could capture. Photographing the moon isn't easy; it's about a thirty-minute procedure on a good night.

As I was focusing the 2,000 mm combo, something rubbed up against my leg. It circled my ankle and my mind pictured a large snake. It's called a knee-jerk reaction. "It" went flying toward the house. A tiny meow came from that direction. Wow, I have a big snake that meows in my front yard. She hid for a second under the deck stairs then came back out to my left leg. This time I saw it, and "it" was a very small kitten. "Okay, kiddo, rub to your heart's content because tonight you will be coyote kibble!" Cats don't last long in the country, not with the number of coyotes out here. I finally got my moon photo and headed inside, wishing this new cat good luck. Hunter met me at the door with Harri right behind him. They followed me to my office and watched me as I edited the pictures. Something was on their minds. I'm very sure they knew that a creature was outside. Living near the end of a dead-end road in the country means people (and I use that term loosely) throw their unwanted pets out of the car on a regular basis. Over the last eleven years, I've taken a couple dozen critters to the animal shelter.

I was leaving for a couple days and as I took my bags to the car. There was the cat at the steps. She ran and rubbed up against my leg again. *"Scat!"* I screamed. I hate cats. The boys sniffed my pant leg when I reentered the house. On my last trip to the car, I had a bowl of water and a small bowl of tuna.

That Night I got a text from Michelle. (My latest wolf sitter) "What's the cat's name?"

"Coyote kibble, I hate cats," I replied.

"But she's so sweet." I didn't reply to that.

Returning two days later, I had purchased some cat food at Walmart to make sure she was alive and healthy for the coyotes. I hate cats. That weekend I hosted a photo shoot for a couple friends, and guess who jumped in? The comments were overwhelming from models and photographers alike.

"What's the cat's name?" over and over again. "It's a girl!" "She's so friendly!"

"Her name is Scat!" I said, and a brief hush fell over the gathering. A week later the weather took a turn for the worse, and predictions were twenty-one degrees Thursday night. My sister carol called to alert me(?) I hate cats. So with the guilt getting to me, I went to the local Walmart and stood in the cat section. Finally a man and his wife grabbed some litter. "Excuse me, do you have a cat?" I stammered. I felt so stupid. At sixty-four years old, I had never had a cat. Did I think they were buying litter for a hazmat situation? I did read that somewhere.

After what seemed to be an hour, they answered smiling, "Yes." I received a quick but informative *Cats for Dummies*, and then they asked if I had any other pets. "She's not a pet. She's just spending some time with me. I hate cats. Sorry, yes, I have a border collie and a wolf."

I wish I had video of their reaction. I'm sure your imagination is better than my vocabulary.

She spent a few cold nights being pampered in the guest bathroom then when I left town again. Michelle introduced everyone for me, and somehow it was all okay while I was gone. Hunter and Harri slept in my room, Hunter on his bed, Harri on mine. Michelle always stays in the guest room, so Scat slept with her. What would the arrangement be when I was home? I once said I'd have a cat when hell freezes over. Hmmm.

HC 42: I SHOULDA NAMED HER ROCKY

When I got home from the road, I wondered how life would be with a wolf, a dog, and a cat. Michele had put Scat in the guest bathroom, so when I entered the house, the first thing I did was let her out. My god! Is her back that itchy or does she love my leg or (dare I say the words) does she love me? I let the boys out and sure enough, there wasn't a war. Hunter seemed to be the most content with the arrangement, just curling up next to me on the couch. Harri just kept looking for the "beast." Being a border collie can take a toll on your heart always being prepared and all. He had seen Scat, and she was smaller than him by a great measure, so he might be able to push her around and get away with it. He was no longer the littlest member of the family, and that had some value to it. After dinner, as I watched TV, it was Hunter to my right and Harri on the floor next to my feet. And Scat? Scat waited till everyone was in place then she jumped up on my left side, sitting half on the top of the couch, half on my shoulder. Funny (because I hate cats) but I felt good about all these changes.

Where had Scat come from? That question swirled around my head as I watched a documentary on Netflix. I live on an unmarked dead end road off another road to nowhere. Hmmm. Someone had dropped her in the country rather than keep her or find her a home. She must have seen my house and headed for the safety of it. If she hadn't, the coyotes would surely have eaten her that first night. Somehow she survived under the deck for a couple weeks before she broke into my heart. I better get her to my vet and have her checked out and spayed ASAP. I decided to do that first thing in the morning, but first there was the question of sleeping arrangements. I could almost see Michele's face as I remembered her words. "Let them work it out."

We made it through the night, luckily, and now as I got out of bed, I wondered where Scat was. Just past my door and Harri took off after Scat, and Scat ran through the living room and Harri was close in pursuit, and the photo equipment all went flying!

Boys to the wolf hotel and Scat to the van, vet time.

It was $366 for a free cat. Maybe that's why "they" dropped her off. Anyway, it gave me a couple days to calm the boys down. When Scat came home, I let her have the run of the house for a while before letting the boys in. Hunter and Harri went right to the laundry room, where Scat was perched on the dryer. Hunter just looked and wagged his tail slowly then headed for my bedroom. Harri was fascinated by Scat, and only when I left did he relax a little. Back in my room, I sat on the edge of my bed. Harri lay on my bed, Hunter on his, and then the usual sounds came from the laundry room. Change, zippers, and buttons clanging in the turning dryer bin. Harri slowly got up and walked to the bedroom door. Listening intently, he began to shake. Slowly he backed up and stood near Hunter for safety. I can only imagine Harri hearing those noises, knowing that Scat was near the dryer. I'll bet he envisioned her punching the dryer like Stallone hit the slab of beef! I shoulda named her Rocky!

HC 43: A HOME INVASION!

Life on the ranch is a series of rituals and habits some would call "routine." Well, on this night we broke a lot of routine and paid the price in adrenaline and sleeplessness. Somewhere around 10:30 p.m. one Friday night, I put some ribs on the smoker and cleaned up that mess and headed for bed. It would be the first night home, and the boys were happy to hit the sack. Usually they sleep on my bed with me on and off through the first night home. I was just feeling the touch of those familiar sheets when I felt the first bite of a fire ant. A rogue ant! No, I said the first! Suddenly I was in real pain, way more than enough to get me up! I would have to surrender for now, a retreat to the guest room. Hunter and a very confused Harri followed me as we left the lights on in my room and headed for safer ground.

Note: lights on, ribs smoking, us in the guest room, and no wolf in the bedroom, sliding door with a doggie door.

I live in Texas on a hundred-acre ranch, and I always have a gun near me. Even in my painful stupor that's one routine I wouldn't break. At 3:35 a.m. I was jolted awake by Hunter's attack noises (really hard to describe because he's usually so calm), Harri barking, *lots of paws* pounding, and screaming!

OMG! I thumbed off the safety on my .45 and walked toward my bedroom, now a battleground! It was (to say the least) a long walk! My mind was was filled with craziness. I pictured a burglar being "treed" by Hunter or maybe just a grizzly bear! I'm glad I left the lights on because there was no doubt that I had to put the safety back on, no shooting these intruders. To my left was Hunter fiercely "punching" a skunk in the rear to negate that weapon and biting fur out as he lunged in and out like a skilled boxer. To my right was Harri in hot pursuit of a second skunk, around and around in a tight circle barking constantly. I knew Hunter was in control for the moment, but maybe I could help Harri and the—wait a minute, as my eyes cleared and focused, he was chasing his own tail! Thank God, we had the situation down to one enemy!

I jumped over the "boxing match" (knocking over Hunter's bed) and opened the sliding glass door all the way. Then I scurried around, closing the two bathroom doors and taking up a position to block any further entrance to the house. The now badly beaten skunk headed for the open door and fell under the deck. Then he tried to run for it. Once in the clear, Hunter killed the skunk instantly. I guess he knew enough from his last encounter to clear the bedroom before killing the invader. I calmed Harri down and praised his bravery. It wasn't an easy event, and the three of us just sat on the couch as a slight smell of skunk lingered in the air. We seemed to all relive that event for about an hour before thoughts of sleep returned. The next morning when I awoke, Harri was at my feet but Hunter was nowhere in sight. I started coffee and walked into my bedroom. He had spent the balance of the night lying in front of the doggy door. Don't mess with Texas!

The Morning after

HC 44: IS HUNTER LIKE A DOG?

The short answer is no. But that wouldn't make for a comprehensive answer or a good chronicle. When I first brought Hunter home in February of 2001, I had a border collie named Jagger. Jagger was the smartest dog I ever had, and he kept smelling Hunter and staring at me. I knew Jagger and I knew the message he was trying to convey. "He's not a dog!" knowing that indeed Hunter was a wolf because I just acquired him from a zoo. Jagger's look was hysterical to me. "Dad! Smell him! He's not a dog!" And when I did smell Hunter, I was unable to suppress the smile. He didn't smell like a dog. Actually, the scent reminded me of a fur pelt at a cabin in Canada when I was seven or eight years old! Smells have a way of magically transporting you to that very time and place where you were. Jagger was a smart dog, but Hunter is a wolf, the grand-ancestor of the dog.

Dog puppies are excited about everything. Hunter was observant of everything going on around him. As soon as he was tall enough, he could (and would) open any door in the house. So how did you keep him in? By making life fun for him so his favorite place was by my side. Strangely enough, it was a mutual feeling. I loved playing with Jagger and Hunter, and soon we had a myriad of undefined "games" we played. Games with no winners or losers and no time limits. Just play till we got tired, then we'd all relax together.

Nothing "sticks" to wolf hair. No burrs or weeds or mulch, nothing, which is a good thing because they are not easy to bathe. I've showered with Hunter and that was a real experience! A skunk got to him, and that event is covered in Hunter chronicle 11

I had an in-home office, so when I was working the phone, Hunter would lie down at my feet. Wolves sleep a lot. I read that as much of eighteen hours a day can be consumed by sleep. That's about right, but when they're awake, they play hard! People who tie their dog to a tree and visit them for food and water are depriving themselves of a real companion. As I write this chronicle, Hunter, Harri, and Scat are on the sofa next to me. If I move to the bedroom, they do the same. The office? You guessed it. Never more than a few feet away. Why? It's a pack thing. A wolf's biggest fear is being alone.

The number one (as in first) question everyone asks is "Aren't you afraid?" It's okay. They really don't know, and I guess the stories and children's books really scared most people. The word *wolves* does sound ominous, and they are certainly powerful enough to "clear the conference room," but that doesn't mean they would. I've had people meet Hunter and love him, play with him, and see his actions. Then later their "friends" convince them that the event was a freak moment and someday the *true wolf* would rise up and eat me for breakfast. I used to get mad, but what difference do they make? None! But I kind of made it a goal to educate the world about the true nature of wolves. In a nutshell, they are either afraid of you and mistrust you or they love you.

I had a complete idiot arguing that "hundreds of people" had been killed by Mackenzie wolves near Yellowstone. His story was told in a convincing manner, and as soon as I saw people with in earshot nodding their heads in agreement, I stood up gave the waiter my credit card and took my dinner to the bar. Oh yes, I did make some rather loud remarks about how stupid this guy would look when everyone googled it. And I hate that expression! It's amazing some people find their way down the birth canal.

What do you feed him? Now that's a legitimate question that I usually answer with "neighbors." After the laugh, I tell the truth. A high-end dog food, Taste of the Wild. The main ingredient is either salmon, bison, or duck, depending on the style. He also loves ham hocks, hot dogs, beef ribs, and pork ribs. He's not a vegetarian at *all*. Oh yes, and the favorite game? Meatball toss!

One of the big differences is that wolves can't bark. Really, they can growl (that's very rare), howl, and have a weird whine, a very high-pitch whine, and "talk." You know that huskies do that part too. It's kinds like Chewbacca in Star Wars.

Is he an indoor or outdoor pet? This question has come up, and frankly I think it's a bit silly. Am I an indoor human or an outdoor human? I think if you have a close relationship with any animal, they will "be" wherever you are. If I'm cooking on the back deck, sipping coffee on the front porch, or watching TV in the living room, Hunter's there with me.

Where does he sleep? Now that's a better question. If I'm sick, hurting, or just upset about something, Hunter sleeps on my bed. He has his own bed with a pillow that says "Hunter." He uses it most of the time.

In summary, he's more loving and more needy than any dog I've ever had. He has nothing to prove to anybody but has amazing strength to back it up if needed. No one has ever dared to hit me with a chair in front of Hunter, so I don't know what he would do. His love is amazing. Last night I woke up, and after it was obvious I wasn't getting back to sleep, I got up, went to the living room to watch some TV, and he was there on the sofa with me. I love my best friend. Yes, that's you Hunter.

HC 45: A ROSE BY ANY OTHER NAME

I've had birthday parties and gone to many. It's a special day, isn't it? The day you were born is the starting point for the hopefully long journey of life. Astrology makes a big deal of it writing totally different traits for people born hours apart. The stars are a huge influence on our destiny, they say. The stars position at that moment determines your destiny. Or do they? Do we live our lives by gliding through a "predetermined" path, reacting certain ways and behaving certain ways because of our astrological signs? Well, what if at fifty years old, we were to find out that there was a mistake and we were a Taurus rather than a Gemini? What if?

And so it was with utmost confidence that I celebrated Hunter's birthday every year. Giving him squeaky toys and chew bones, new collars and pillows for his bed. He was a Christmas baby! December 25, 2000! A bunch of wolves had been born on Christmas day at Arbuckle Wilderness Drive-Through Zoo. When he was at two weeks old, a brutal ice storm hit, and the wolf pups had been gathered and taken to the main building. There they would be safe and fed goat's milk and pampered by the workers until they were old enough to be sold. By law, the pups had to be sold because their "pen" was too small to house any more than Mom and Pop.

I got this from the girl at the visitors' center when I bought Hunter. She had said, "He's five weeks old today! Today is the first day we can sell him. Do you really want him?" Then came the now-famous conversation that ended with me carrying a wolf to my car and driving back to Dallas with Mr. Baby Wolf crawling across the console again and again to be on my lap. But thinking back to the "rest of the story," I had asked what his birthday was. The excited staff member (maybe sixteen years old) said, "Well, he's five weeks old today, so with that, she flipped back the calendar, mumbling numbers to herself. "Oh my God!" said exclaimed. "He's a Christmas baby." I thought to myself, *That's easy to remember.*

And so it was on that cold day in February that that baby wolf was proclaimed a "Christmas baby," thereby born on December 25 in the year of our Lord 2000. Hear ye, hear ye and all that. Every year I celebrated Hunter's birthday on December 25 alongside of Christmas. Now I share my birthday with Grace Kelly, Neil Young, and Charlie Manson for what that's worth, but Hunter shared it with divinity! No Charlie Mansons tainting the star-destined future for him!

Joy filled the air on every one of Hunter's birthdays until he got about twelve and still looked very young. Was I looking through "rose-colored" glasses? How old do wolves live?

I stopped in to Garold Wayne Zoo and inquired. I was greeted by an older "ranger" type gentleman. Even all those years later, I was worried that if I told him the Hunter story, he would grab me, screaming that I couldn't buy that wolf and they had searched everywhere for me and arrest me and take my "son" away. I would be clever and ask what the price of a ticket was and pretend that the price was more than I could spare then ask a few questions.

"Eight dollars per car?" I said. "I'll come back with my whole family then." As if I had a family!

Then I began to beat around the bush. "How many wolves do you have? Where do you get them? What colors are they? How old are they?" He had answered every question in stride, so now was my time to pop the big one. "How old do wolves live?"

He stopped in his tracks and looked me square in the eyes and said, "I don't know." Yes, another bad moment in my plan. I thought I may never know as the Internet provided conflicting information.

That was that until about a year or two ago, I ran across a wolf forum. A real expert answered that question and it's amazing.

In captivity, like Hunter's parents: three to five years! In the wild? "We think ten to twelve years at best." My heart sank then. In the care of humans and living for the purpose of caring for that human family or pack, with no young ones coming up to take their rank in the pack? Seventeen to twenty years! Now that's what I wanted to hear! So I pulled up Hunter's "first-day picture" and checked the metadata on the digital picture. I got him on February 11, 2001, so at the time, I said he's thirteen and going strong with years to go! *Yay!*

A few weeks ago, I was telling the story of acquiring Hunter and how silly stupid the young female staff member had been when I wondered, how stupid was she? The metadata was rigidly undeniable, so I counted back five weeks from February 11 and my jaw hit the floor. Hunter was born on January 7, 2001, the year of our Lord! Yeah yeah yeah, oh my, I had celebrated the wrong day for all these years. Was I afraid to tell him? Yes, I was. I don't know why but I was. So I write this tonight to announce to Hunter and the world tomorrow, 1-7-2016, that his real birthday is January 7! He will get ribs and a squeaky toy and an apology from me. He's fifteen years old today! Does it matter? I'll leave that to a much better writer than I. "Would a Rose, by any other name, smell as sweet?" Yes, William, it would.

HC 46: A FAMILY THAT PLAYS TOGETHER

Scat was beginning to "sharpen" her nails on the leather couch. The word *declawed* sounds so weird, but the vet said it was common and the right thing to do. So now I've got about $600 into my free cat. Oh well. She was so happy to get home from the vet, *but* yes! Hunter and Harri went nuts to get her back. I think that at thirteen years old, Hunter needs a form of inside entertainment, and Scat is just that. In his earlier days, he would run and chase the donkeys for a couple hours then cool off his feet. He never wanted to catch them because that wasn't the game. When they slowed up, he would too. It was fun to watch, but the last couple years, he just hasn't been interested.

Scat's presence brought a playful side to the ranch. Hunter watches her and wags his tail as she gets close and kisses his nose. I should quit my job and just photograph this crew.

She was very afraid of Hunter at first (God knows why). She was kind of put off by his visits to her bathroom. Being a beta wolf, he just had to check on her on a regular basis. That would entail a "walk through" of the guest bedroom that houses her kitty litter and her bowl on the sink where I place a packet of tuna every day. Several times she would see him enter the bathroom and sneak up to the door to see what he was doing. He'd go about the inspection without a care. Look around, sniff, general inspection of her private quarters. A couple times he would exit and they would be nose to nose for a second, then Scat would Scat! Fear is a funny emotion. It inhibits us and divides us.

When word processing first took hold of our lives, I copied a section of the Bible and replaced the word *Satan* with the word *fear*. It actually was a better read! I felt that if she would stop being afraid of Hunter, the family would be a tighter unit. Hunter? I could tell he liked her a lot. He was never jealous of the time I spent holding her or having her on my lap while we all watched TV. I just needed to make Scat realize that *if* Hunter was a threat, she wouldn't have lasted a second! Well, those are the right words are they?

She likes playing with "things," mostly the pull knobs on window blinds. Not good. So I saw this ad on TV for a cat toy, Cat's Meow. It looked like it would occupy her time and give the blinds a break!

If you've ever order something from a TV ad, you know what I mean. "But wait, there's more!" All in all I guess it took close to twenty minutes to order this thing, and by the time I hung up, I had purchased six or so of the deluxe model! Oh yes, and I had upgraded the shipping to make it get here in a reasonable amount of time.

If you have a cat, buy one or six! It is a crazy "sweeping ball" that circles around underneath a cloth cover. Scat didn't just have a new toy, she had a babysitter! As soon as I turned it on, she was hooked, and then the sound hit the ears of Hunter and Harri. They knew the seductive sound of a squeaky toy, but this was different, and the sound of Scat's paws and her jumping/pouncing on the new toy was too much for them.

Her concentration wasn't to be broken, but Harri and Hunter circled the ongoing festivities as if cheering Scat on to victory. The picture says what I can't in words, so I hope you enjoy it. Since the new toy is battery operated, I have quite a stack of "C" cells waiting for duty. It was well worth the aggravating phone call because everyone plays a little closer these days. I think the fear of Hunter has subsided and the family/pack is a little tighter. The Cat's Meow has done a great job at helping love conquer all.

HC 47: THE WIFE BARK

I guess some of you noticed that Dottie kind of left the story. She lives with my sister about fifteen minutes away. I love her immensely, and when I visit, she is "all over me." So why? She's a lady that just has to be the boss of the family, so she would just lean in to Hunter's left ear and bark the shrill and piercing bark that I nicknamed the wife bark. I haven't met a woman who liked that expression nor a man who doesn't understand exactly what I mean. To me there is a greeting bark, a "Let's play" bark, a "Who's there?" bark, even an "I love you" bark. Then there is "the wife bark." I bought a little speaker thing that was supposed to detect a bark then screech so loud that it hurt and the dog would never bark again. Whoever invented this thing never met Dottie. I'd come home, Hunter would jump up on his fence, Dottie would bark in his ear, then the machine would screech and Dottie would bark at the machine! It would screech; she would bark. Bad Idea.

I had some friends suggest a muzzle, but that just seems cruel.

It wasn't just me that "the bark" upset. It was Hunter and Harri! When Dottie would bark at Hunter, he would whine and run away.

So, I just couldn't kick Dottie out, and my sister Carol came to the rescue. Carol had three dogs already, and Dottie could rule the roost because the three were older and way more passive. Every time I visit my sister (usually every week), Dottie goes crazy with love! She jumps on me, and yes, about once a month, she spends two to three nights at the ranch. Usually after three days, she begins the "wife bark" and I return her to Carol's house. I love them all, but a relaxed family is a happy family.

More people are visiting me these days, and I suspect that one of the great motivators is the knowledge that, you got it. Rick lives with a wolf!

One of my closest friends from high school is Jack Fowle. We met in the eighth grade and became instant friends, and I jumped into music; he just kept studying. He went into public service and climbed to the top echelon of the EPA. After his retirement a few years ago, he joined the private sector, working heavily with the government, serving as a consultant.

When he called last month and said he would be visiting Dallas, I was thrilled. We met at his hotel in Dallas. I wondered why Jack was at a convention with all these young chemists. *Duh!* He was a guest lecturer of course. He came to the ranch, and when Hunter met him, it was amazing. Hunter must have sensed the deep and long lasting friendship. Scat and Hunter smothered Jack with love and attention. How wonderful it is to have an old friend visit and made to feel so welcome. I even took Jack by my sister's house so he could meet Dottie and hear for himself the wife bark.

HC 48: LOOKING FOR A WOLF MODEL

This sounds like a simple task because everyone who meets Hunter wants pictures with him. No offense to any of my female friends, but I want a really exotic-looking woman who is a professional model and is thrilled to be with Hunter. Someone fragile looking to show that Hunter means no harm. I need someone small to emphasize Hunter's size.

Now you're getting the picture. One of my close friends is a twenty-one–year-old budding model. Sounds good? She's almost six feet tall and makes Hunter look like a dog of about 60 pounds. He's 122 pounds, and I want that to come across in the photo. So the search goes on. There are a whole cult of people who do a thing called "cosplay." From what I gather, they get together at conventions all dressed up and *love* to be photographed. Hmmm. There must be someone in this crowd that would fit the bill.

I attended the Dallas Comic Con for three years, A-Kon for two years, Anime for two years, Fan Fest for two years. Really fun and lovely people. I took thousands of pictures of these people in costumes that must have taken hours on time and a lot of money to construct. No one stood out.

Then I attended the Dallas Comic Con 2014 at the Irving Convention Center. My nephew told me the "red carpet" would be at 3:00 p.m., but a special shoot of female heroes was scheduled for 11:00 a.m., and he was really excited to see what the reproduction of some famous (in this world) painting would look like. The girls started gathering and to me; they all dressed the same. White evening gown, heels, and I guess the wigs were a tip-off as to what superstar they were. There she was, standing with a few other participants but so exotic! She looked like a blond Audrey Hepburn. I walked up to her and motioned to my camera. I hoped the lens could capture her essence. I snapped one shot and smiled as I looked at the LCD screen. "Perfect," I said, "and I knew it would be." She smiled and thanked me for taking her picture. Where else do you get free models to pose then thank you! Some fifteen girls/women posed for the recreation. After a few minutes, I was convinced she was the one, *and* she stood under 5 feet with heels. I had to ask. I was sure she'd think me a nut but I had to ask. "Excuse me, but I've been looking for just the right model to pose." She looked at me with doubt. "With my wolf." This amazing face exploded with joy. "Oh my God, I've been searching the Internet for a wolf I could pose with!"

She grabbed a piece of paper and started writing down her e-mail address as her friends were telling her (rightfully so) that she had no idea who I was. I guess she had the same feeling that I did. It was a good thing. When I got home that night, I swear Hunter was excited about the idea as I showed him the picture of Chelsea. Chelsea and I exchanged a few e-mails, and because she was twenty years old, her mom wanted to come out with her when she met Hunter. It was classic Hunter—he hopped up on the sofa between Chelsea and her mom. He kissed Mom right off the bat then snuggled with her as she exclaimed with joy what a gentleman he was. Then Hunter shifted his attention to Chelsea and kissed her from the knees to the face. She couldn't stop smiling; she had found her wolf. I had found my model.

Then she posted the wolf pictures I took. Her friends all started telling her stories about how wolves just suddenly go wild! The stories were all "I read somewhere," "My cousin said," "I manage a pet store and…" Well, all of a sudden, no more e-mails. Oh well, you can lead a horse to drink, but sometimes the pictures don't turn out!

HC 49: THE PHARAOHS HAD IT EASY!

So Moses has a tough time (to say the least) and gets God to change the pharaoh's thinking.

The rivers turn to blood, it rains frogs, gnats and flies—*so what*? Boils, hail, and locusts! Is that all you got? Darkness and sick animals? That's a walk in the park! Do what to the firstborn? Now that is an attention grabber.

Why do I write this? Why is it even on my mind? Because the Sunday before Easter this year (yeah, Passover) began the annual plague here at the ranch. Springtime and it's the shedding season. Had Moses and God unleashed this, nothing else would have had to be done. The pharaoh would have thrown in the towel in a day!

I've had dogs all my life and I have seen shedding. My mom used to shave the dogs so the hair that fell would at least be shorter. You're thinking, "I know what you mean." No, you don't. Every morning during the season of demonic hair, I brush Hunter for twenty minutes in hope (futile as it is) of stemming the tide of white fur. I brush out enough fur to fill a trash can! Yes, "a dog a day" is how I refer to it! Still, as Hunter walks away, the contrail of hair follows him.

I woke up Easter morning, and Hunter had curled up the night before on one of my shirts—a formerly black shirt. I posted the picture on Facebook and had over a hundred comments! I was warning friends not to wear dark colors; most listened but those who didn't were screaming like fearful pharaohs. "Let my purple go!"

Do wolves in the wild do this? I can't imagine it. How could it get by the EPA?

One morning "after" the brushing, Hunter hopped off my bed. A clump of fur just shot out of him and played in the turbulent air of the ceiling fan. Scat just watched it's random journey intently as only a cat can. What was this floating object? Aha! An unidentified floating object! What would the Air Force say about this phenomenon? I can see the headlines: "They Come in Pieces."

The one good side effect of this is he doesn't run away! He's a smart boy and knows I could easily follow the fur to *wherever* he went. Maybe he just doesn't want the donkeys laughing at him!

The plague has gotten worse, and I know I have several more weeks of torture, but how does Hunter feel about this? What is he thinking? After the first couple weeks, he seems embarrassed. The photos I normally take of him (all the time) have ceased. He must feel neglected or ugly because I can see an ashamed twinge in his expressions. He walks with his head hung low.

In five to six weeks, he will again walk with pride; his head will be held high again, his follicles holding on to the hair. But the time seems to stop. I know it doesn't but perception is reality.

I know I should stop whining, and I know it will end in the joy of the summer coat. But every night after sweeping (the vacuum cleaner resigned), I lay down my head and think, *The pharaohs had it easy.*

HC 50: A STROKE OF LUCK!

After surviving the shedding season of 2014, I thought I was ready for anything and quietly hoping for an uneventful summer. Hunter, Harri, and Scat were actually playing together and even sleeping together. Believe it or not, everyone sleeping on my bed was now the norm. I took pictures of the crew and posted them on Facebook, but something began nagging at me. Hunter had taken the role of the beta wolf, the nursemaid, and "true to form," he was an independent member of a closely knit family (pack). He slept in his bed every night—well, every night I was healthy and feeling well. Whenever I had a surgery or severe injury, he slept next to me on my bed. Call me slow, but it wasn't obvious to me for weeks that the only thing wrong in this scenario was that I wasn't sick, or was I? I had hurt my back in April and it was getting worse every day, but I had to travel for my job. Ignoring the pain, I continued till I needed a cane. Then as it got worse, I was given a walker and a wheelchair from my sister. The walker I used, but I drew the line at using the wheelchair. In the movie *Shawshank Redemption*, there's a line—"Get busy living or get busy dying"—and I wasn't going to let myself get to the wheelchair level. The walker was hard enough, and I learned that all my bathroom doorways were one inch narrower than the walker forcing you to do a weird "twist and shuffle" cha-cha.

I did notice that visitor traffic was down that spring and summer! Friends whom I was looking forward to seeing would cancel the visit when they heard a wasn't "feeling well." That really hurt because that's when you need someone to visit. My sister was a constant help and took the load off Hunter. Cooking, cleaning, TV, and most of all, worrying about the unspoken. Was this the rest of my life?

I attended a convention in Las Vegas and of course went in two days early so I could do some helicopter tours of the Grand Canyon. I was tired all day. At the end of each day, I was exhausted. That word gets overused, but I was drained, as in nothing left in the tank but fumes. Then the convention started and I rented a scooter/wheelchair because I couldn't stand up and endure the back pain. On the third morning, as I began to tell the taxi driver my destination, did I have a stroke? It had to be a stroke; my lips weren't working. I was convinced Hunter had known it was coming. I couldn't speak and everything was in a fog. I knew what I wanted to say, but my lips were slow and confused. To say it was scary would be an understatement.

Sunrise Hospital in Las Vegas. They immediately did a blood workup, and my hemoglobin count was 5. Nothing showed up on the MRIs or CT scans. *But* My hemoglobin count (15–17 is normal, 12 is anemic) was 5! I was given two units of blood. Now I'm thinking there probably isn't a worse place in the world to get blood than Las Vegas! Somehow I knew it wasn't a stroke; I was dead. They warned me that I would die from the pressure change on an airplane, and sis was ready come get me! *But* they hadn't found any evidence of a stroke! I was not going to be convinced that I had a stroke. I was "just bleeding to death." No problem, I can deal with that. I think.

I signed myself out on Saturday and flew home. I know, *way* against the rules but that is and always will be me. I was sure my head wouldn't "explode on takeoff." However confident I was, if the lady next to me would have spilled her bloody mary on takeoff, well, you know. My sister met me at the airport, got me home, and stayed for the next two months. An upper IG showed a bleeding ulcer was the culprit. Then appropriate time of building up the stats till I had laser spine surgery. What a miracle procedure! Coming home was like a reunion. Hunter was crazed with excitement; Dad was walking again.

I am writing this two weeks postsurgery, and although I am still in rehab for another six weeks, the family is whole and healthy again. Hunter, Scat, and Harri follow me everywhere, and we are wrestling again and playing with squeaky toys. No trace of the stroke shows up on the MRI, and my speech has returned to normal. Everyone plays on my bed, and I am so grateful for everything I have. Last night I watched the moonrise from the back deck. Everyone sat there silently. I imagine we were all thanking God for all that had transpired as well as the final outcome. After all the procedures, I am being reminded again how blessed I am—in this case, more than a stroke of luck.

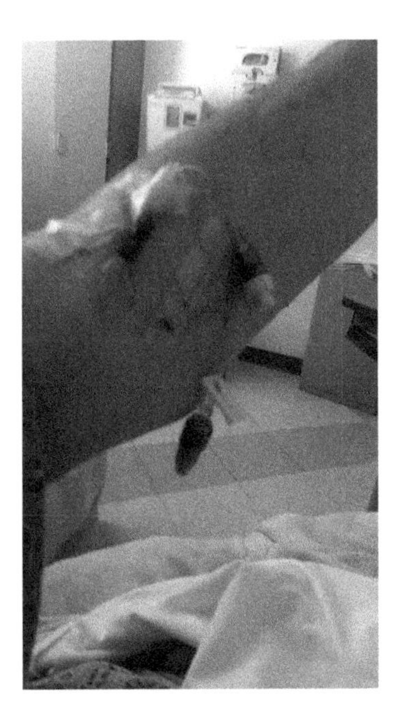

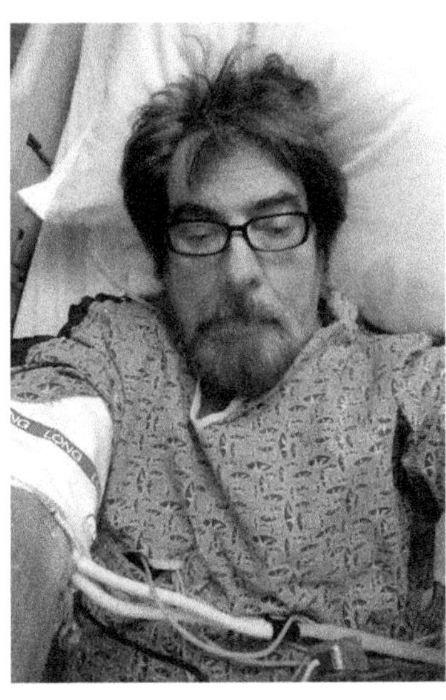

HC 51: SOMETHING SIMPLE

Every year at this time (Halloween), I look at Hunter and remember our first year out here on the ranch. For those of you who have followed the chronicles, it's a funny memory. For those who joined the chronicles after number 10, I dressed Hunter up in a duck outfit that year and took a series of pictures. When I looked at them on my computer, I knew I had been a *bad dad*! Wolves have more muscles in their face than dogs. Often when I have a guest, they think they can read Hunter's mind because his expressions are so clear. Well, that day his expression was very clear. *Take this off me!* I promised him I'd never do that again, and I haven't. However, I was cleaning out some junk drawers a few years ago, and I grabbed the duck outfit. As soon as Hunter saw the costume, he ran from my side and off to the bedroom. You have to understand that Hunter is by my side *all* the time we are together. When I wake, he's the first to greet me at the edge of my bed, stands by me as I brush my teeth, etc. He moves from the kitchen to the living room to the home office as my protecting shadow. So for him to run to another room, he remembers!

This year has been unusual for many health and travel reasons. I have spent more time at home this year than ever before. Has being home changed my relationship with Hunter? Yes, he's happier and seems to sleep more soundly. While I was hampered with back and blood issues, he hovered gently over me. Now that the back surgery went well and he sees me walking, he bumps into be like a playful brother. Of course, at his size, I go flying every now and then.

He, Harri, and Scat all play like crazy people for hours. When the lights go out, the tempo slows down and Hunter kisses everyone before lying down for the night. He has fully accepted Scat as a family member, something that I wasn't sure would happen. I'm getting used to being wrong. I think it suits me quite well. Another stray began to "hang out" on and around the front deck. When she would meow, Scat would pull up close to me on the couch. Hunter would then stand at the front door and growl in an attempt to scare the stranger away. After a few days, I took the cat up to the animal shelter, noting that she had been declawed and was wearing a flea collar. This was no throwaway. Sure enough, the lady at the shelter said they had been having a lot of calls about a lost cat matching her description! That day ended well for everyone.

With Winter coming on, so does the snuggle times with the crew. Friday nights by the fireplace, just hanging, one of the simplest things you can imagine. Sharing time with the ones you love—simple yet something to be cherished as sacred and holy. I hope you read this and say, "Wow, Hunter didn't do anything *big* this issue, except something simple"—the simple fact that we all have ones we love. Humans or animals, hopefully you have both in your life. The simple fact is, we should not assume that the hugs and kisses are there and will continue forever. We have to realize how special each moment is in the scheme of things. It is something wonderfully grand—something as simple as love.

HC 52: A SUMMER SCARE

It's August in Texas and that means hot. I put one of those bamboo shades on Hunter's pen (better known as La Quinta Lobo), *but* it's 109 degrees and that is just crazy. By the way, the weather channel measures the temperature in the shade, so add another ten to twelve degrees. He's got water and his "cool" trough for cooling down, but I'm a worrier. I got a call from a supplier, and he asked about a sample I have stored downtown in my building. Does it have bolts or nubs on the cabinet? I don't know, but the building is five minutes away, so I told him I'd check. I looked at the boys. Hunter and Harri were stretched out on the wood floor in the main hallway (the coolest place in the house). I hated to put them in the pen for such a short trip. I slipped out the door, went to the warehouse, and called Joel. Bolts on the side! That was good news. He asked a few questions more then I left. Fire trucks that I avoided by taking a different route that took me by the hardware store. I need more dog food. Another stop. OMG, my meds were ready and soon the delay was pretty long. But I was leaving for DFW for a couple days, seeing dealers, and I had to get this done. When I drove up, Harri was running around in the front yard! He was half *mud*, so he must have gone to the pond. No, there was the front yard's picket fence, so the mud must have been from crawling under the house. I expected to see Hunter still sleeping when I entered the house. Nope. When they woke, they must have panicked when they figured out I was gone. Being alone is a wolf's biggest fear, and Harri feeds off anything! I put Harri in the pen just as he was about to jump on my bed. Close call for the sheets! I went back to the front porch. I just stood there and tried to think of Hunter and how he would react. Where would he go trying to find me? So many times I've left for the store and had people stay and be with Hunter. They said he got pretty crazy when he heard the car leave the ranch. Then I heard the panting. He was near. I ran off the porch to look under the house, and there he was, facing away from me, panting and seemingly unable to get up. He turned and looked at me with glazed eyes and a shaking paw. Slowly I turned his 120-pound body and nudged him toward me. He could not stand up at first, but slowly I calmed him down and he tried and tried. Each attempt I would have to console him and calm him down from a panicked state of mind. Finally he was almost facing me, and I helped him up with my outstretched arms and we walked/stumbled inside. I rubbed his head with cold water and he drank and drank. Oh yes, and I was getting a lot of wolf kisses. I texted Paul (my brother-in-law) as he was in Commerce, getting a physical. He stopped by and replaced the skirting boards that the panicking Hunter had ripped off to get to me. In his panic, he quickly got overworked, and in this heat, that's bad. Once inside, Hunter staggered over to the living room to lie on the cold floor. I checked out Hunter and found that what I thought were injuries were just marks from his panic escape. It took forever before he began to breath normally. Soon I was calm enough to take pictures and relax with my boys. Harri had cleaned off in the cooling tub and quickly dried off in this heat. I let him in from the pen. Everything was good again, but we all had a summer scare.

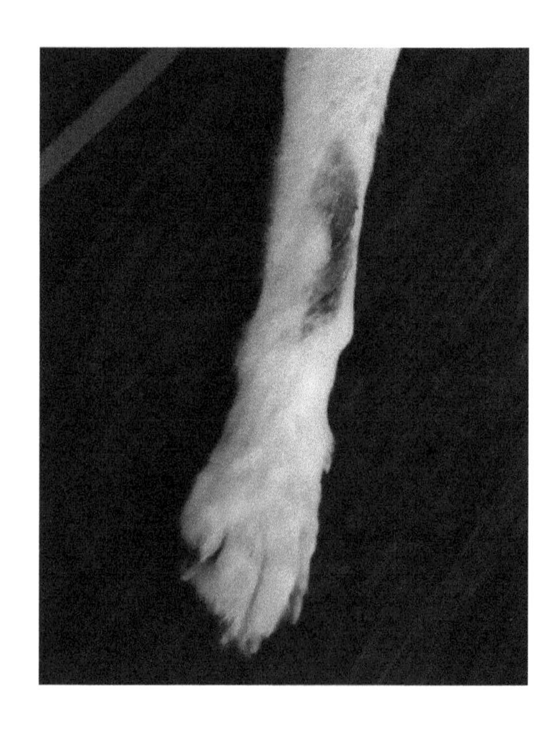

HC 53: JULY 4 WEEKEND 2012

My very close friend Michael Ciravolo (president of Schecter Guitars), his wife, Tish (president of Daisy Rock Guitars), and their two teenage daughters (Sophia, twelve, and Nicole, fourteen) stopped in on their way from LA to Disney World to share Michael's birthday on Saturday. Friday at 6:00 p.m. till Sunday at 9:00 a.m, we rocked!

These days it's more common to see a family eating in a restaurant, all of them texting friends and checking out the social media sights. Well, Michael Ciravolo and I have been friends for a while, and a couple years ago, he stopped by for a taste of the ranch and, of course, to meet Hunter. Hunter's a great judge of character, so he fell for Michael immediately. Hunter loves "guy" weekends; it's a chance to meet someone new, play, and show off his skills. Michael and I took a jeep ride at about two thirty in the morning, and we got a surprise. A gang of coyotes ran past the jeep like a scene from Jurassic Park! Of course, we both had guns, and that was a bit of a surprise to the coyotes. The headlights don't work on my jeep, but we were wearing military night vision, so everything is green and black and the barrel flash a burst of white. There is no way I can describe what we saw, so just let your imagination fill in the gaps. At the end of that visit, Michael said he would return with the whole family. People say a lot of things but he meant it. A couple years later, he requested his present be a family trip to rancho rico. The Fourth of July fest in Allen that year had the Bangles playing, and Tish is old friends with them, so a message that she was present was all that was needed to get to the backstage after their performance while the fireworks popped over the stage and all of us! They are a fun group, and *yes*, they had me walking like an Egyptian. We got back late and launched our own

Chinese sky lanterns, and of course, everyone played with Hunter. He loved the upbeat girls, and he was in heaven with the visitors. The next day was more ATV riding and shooting and general ranch play. I loaded a Class III Tec-9 (full auto) I have with twenty-one bullets so Michael could give himself a birthday twenty-one-gun salute. That was over quickly, but everyone had a laugh. Jeep driver's education was pretty wild as the girls didn't know how to drive a stick, but you can't hurt *anything* on the ranch. They did love the ATVs (no gears to deal with). That night we tried more fun toys. The night vision has another cool use, stargazing. If you ever get your hands on a pair and they are the real stuff, look up. There are a thousand infrared stars to every white one! It's actually startling. The first time I looked up, I was amazed at how little "space" was left!. That started a long conversation and *big* questions that just seem to stem from feeling so small. It was a busy weekend of relaxed fun. Everyone should do weekends like this.

I wish you could have been here. We had a ball.

ATVs, sunsets, animals, stargazing, night vision fun, fireworks, shooting photos, and guns and photos *of* guns. Dealey Plaza, a Bangles concert (backstage passes were involved), lantern launching, rocket launching, teenage driver's ed, and *laughing*! They left and I slept for thirteen hours!

His girls didn't touch their cell phones all weekend, and they loved it!

WANTED

"Michael got to give himself a 21 gun salute! .9 Sec.

You Had To Be Here!"

HC 54: THE WOLF DECORATOR RETIRES

Some things don't have to be said, but somehow when they are spoken aloud. They become tangible and become a living breathing entity to be reckoned with, a manifestation to be dealt with, a danger to my calm life.

Hunter's getting older. There, I said it but, so am I, so is my house, my car, even the coffee I brewed this morning. He's having a hard time with his hips and getting up and down, on and off my bed, the sofa, even his bed. He sleeps a lot more than he used to. Maybe he has to. Or maybe it's the only pleasure-based thing besides eating that aging hasn't stolen from him. Maybe it's a great place to go. You see, in his dreams I'm sure he breaks out of the fence and chases donkeys and llamas and swims in the pond to the chagrin of the horses and armadillos. Hell, he probably drives the jeep when he dreams. When he returns (wakes up), he's lying safely on the rug, sofa, or my bed: safe, rested, and ready for another adventure in dreamland.

I truly don't understand the thought process behind the action of putting a pet in a cage or tied to a tree with a chain. It seems that many people think that way. I have seen many dogs tied to a tree, and at 6:00 p.m. they receive their bowl of food and a water refill. I could never do that, but I cannot judge those who do. So why does Hunter have a pen? Because his separation anxiety is so great, so strong, that he has seen me drive to the back fields in the jeep and jumped through the window pane onto the deck to "be with Dad." Once as I drove on the "path" to the horses (a long and looping half mile), he took the shortcut through the woods and greeted me at the horses' feeding trough, his tongue hanging out and his tail wagging, so happy with himself and his escape run.

To clarify, his "pen" is 42 feet long by 16 feet wide (672 square feet), and as I was designing/building it to be "wolf proof," he sat and watched my every move. Every Screw into every plank every piece of chain link was scrutinized by him. I listened to the radio as I worked. "Our suites in Acapulco are a spacious 700 square feet in size!" I grinned and looked at Hunter. "Did you hear that? I'm building you a suite, not a pen. Dogs have pens, but a wolf deserves a suite!"

He only occupies the La Quinta Lobo when I go to the store my sister's house or travel overnight on business. The ranch sitter follows the same protocol, and it's for his protection and it's comfortable. You have to understand when Hunter panics, all bets are off. Once when he was younger, a sitter left him in the house, locked the door to the backyard, and left Jagger in the backyard. Here's the result of this miscalculation.

And so it was that this visual memory haunted me as I needed to leave for town, a visit to the sight of my new occupational adventure. But I saw Hunter fast asleep on my office couch, where I had been planted for a long time. Harri just followed me everywhere and seemed to be expecting the call "Come on, boys! Gotta go to work," which meant they would head for La Quinta Lobo and I would be gone for an undetermined amount of time. I looked at that wolf I love so much and tried to determine his abilities and attitude at this age. I needed to trust him, but I would not surprise him with me being gone. I wrapped my arms around him kissed him and told him I would only be gone for a short while and I would return to feed him a lunch snack. After the comments, he put his head down and watched me disappear from the room, and I'm sure he listened as the car started and drove off. But I had told him where I was going and when I'd be back.

Two hours later, I wrapped up the show and tell with Brad Davis at the "arts co-op" and headed home, and the monsters of my mind rose from their slumber and paid me a visit. Number 1, Hunter could have jumped through the window pane as he had eleven years ago, but as long as he wasn't cut and bleeding, he couldn't jump the picket fence these days and would be in the front yard. Number 2, Hunter and Harri together could have pulled a fence board lose and escaped, and the horses could have chased them and they couldn't get back in. *Nah!* Number 3, they did panic and "redecorated" the blinds again. Each scenario grew in my mind, and as I neared the ranch, I sped up until I stopped and ran through the picket fence gate and up the stairs. I opened the door and Hunter and Harri—yes, and even Scat—were within feet of the door, happy to see me but relaxed and calm. And the house was intact. I guess my wolf redecorator has retired. Older and more appreciative of our humble dwelling, they were just happy, and so am I. I am returning to town after lunch, but I think I'll go back to the regular routine in case this trip takes longer. The important thing is we have set a new realm of freedoms and trust, and that's a good thing. Embrace the changes to come.

HC 55 RETURN TO EDEN

It's been fifteen years. Wow, that is so hard to believe. It was February 11, 2001 and like my usual self, I just did it with no thought whatsoever. I put down the American Express on the counter at Arbuckle Wilderness Animal Drive-Through Zoo. What did I get for $200? A little creature that had no idea about anything except that he loved the taste of goat's milk and it made him sleepy. During sleep he would ask himself questions about all the basics, and I'm sure his biggest question at five weeks old was "What's next?" I bought a milk crate at the Walmart in Ardmore, Oklahoma, and he seemed happy because that's what his world was behind the counter of the welcome area. Now, fifteen years later, Hunter and I can both look back at what was next. What an adventure! We rolled and played as the other dogs in the house sniffed. Not a dog. Smell him! He's not a dog. Well, he wasn't. He was a wolf, and we had begun a journey into the totally unknown world of prejudice, ignorance (no stones being thrown here because I was totally ignorant about wolves in the wild, never mind living with one), inquiring minds, and most of all, laws.

Technically, Hunter, being a wolf, was classified as an aggressive animal. But why? Where was the evidence? Where were the mauling reports? Where were the "death by wolf" reports? Where were the missing people suspected of being killed by wolves? As I found out, the only place you could read about this sort of aggression was in the fairy tale section of the library. But the laws were real. You can't have a wolf as a pet, really. Okay, well, not really. You can if he's part dog. Now this is getting stupid. A wolf that isn't aggressive has to have "dog" in his family to become a nonaggressive animal. *But* dogs *can* and do become aggressive. And they aren't as smart. So if you dumb down an amazing animal by breeding it, you *can* have it as a pet? Wolves have two emotions toward humans—they are either afraid of you or they are your friend. Some of the smarter vets just look the other way and register the baby wolves as malamutes, and everyone is happy.

So (getting back to the story) yesterday my work took me right up I-35 in Oklahoma, right by exit 51 and the birthplace of my baby Hunter. I left early so I could see the new wolves and maybe just *maybe* see some of Hunter's family tree. It was a weekday, and so they shouldn't be too busy and maybe I could have a really cool visit. "Not busy" is an understatement; they were *empty*!

I walked up the steps, half-wondering if they were open at all. The door was open and the lobby was warm and inviting. I had butterflies! I was so excited to learn all I could about Hunter's family. Where had they sold his brothers and sister? A pleasant young lady was behind the counter asking "How many people? Do you want to buy food for the animals?" Surprised that they were open and it was business as usual, I just blurted out, "Where are the wolves? How many do you have?"

"We haven't had wolves in years." Then a long moment later. "My God, are you all right, sir?"

HC 56: ANOTHER HEALTH SCARE

Joe Louis was interviewed after he lost (by knockout) to Rocky Marciano. "I knew where to punch, the openings were there. I knew the combinations that would destroy him. My body just didn't respond to me. The openings just came and went."

Typical Saturday-morning joy and treat sausages and belly rubs. Life is grand at the ranch. Sure, Hunter is getting older and has needed a heavy push to help him get on the bed at night. Jenny (you'll learn about her in the next chronicle) has helped Hunter (122 pounds) get up on the couch to watch TV with us. I remember when Buffy (my first border collie) would slip on the tiles and scream from the pain of her hind legs not supporting her anymore. She was eighteen. we went to the vet and he put her on steroids. In a week, she was a puppy again. A shot every six weeks and she was so happy. Good quality of life *but* steroids wreck the kidneys and liver, and after three years, she went to sleep by the pool, never to wake from her peaceful rest. Twenty-one years, *wow*! I felt then and still do that I did the right thing for her. After all, she was playing ball and fetching for three more years with no hint of suffering.

I put off making that switch to steroids because I can't stand the thought that even in three years, I may lose Hunter. Selfish? Yep. And so it was that morning that I was talking on the phone and the boys wanted more to do, Hunter and Harri broke out to have a morning donkey chase. Like so many times before, Hunter would find a "weak spot," a loose or rotted old board in the house skirting. The crawl under the house is an easy one. I'm sure their adventuresome hearts sank when they saw the picket fence. Hunter no longer had the strength and skill to cleanly hop over a picket fence. Harri, a follower by nature, had never tried. In his glory days, Hunter could easily clear the six foot privacy fence in the backyard (till I put a hot wire above the fence).

After a perimeter walk, I'm sure Hunter noticed that the old spring on the gate no longer closed it all the way. The kids were loose! They ran or most likely trotted to the nearest pond. Some two hundred yards away from the house. By that time I noticed the "lack of company" and headed out in pursuit.

My jeep didn't start, so the van would be my means of locating them. It didn't take long. The sound of the engine let the boys know I was looking. In the old days, that was the start of an adventure, and we would run the ranch till Hunter's feet got tired and we'd soak in a pond (I have four) then head home with glorious memories. Not today. Harri was actually in the lead heading home and toward the van, Hunter walking slowly behind. As soon as I exited the van, Harri jumped in and I walked toward Hunter. He just looked up and "expressed" that a run wasn't going to happen today. He looked sad and strangely old. I attached his leash for no particular reason and, realizing he needed the lower entrance of the sliding door, opened it.

That's when the thunder started. I could feel it then I heard it, the thunderous roar of my nine horses racing closer. I didn't have to look. I *knew* I had to get Hunter in the van. I wrapped my arms around his waist and lifted. My god, he was heavy, but the adrenaline kicked in (yes, I was sore later) and he fell in the door and onto the floor of the van as I closed the door.

I know you've seen the Wild West shows where the Indians circle around the covered wagons, terrorizing the settlers. They learned that attack plan from horses. The horses, all horses, have an instinct to stomp wolves and coyotes, and that instinct was kicked into full gear as they sensed the weak and helpless Hunter. The picture does not capture the "frenzy" of the moment. I am *not* afraid of horses and I do love them, but I was afraid of what they could do to Hunter, what they would do to Hunter given the chance. If that event takes place, all I could do would be watch my beloved Hunter as he was trampled to death in front of me. *That* scared me as I drove the van.

Hunter, clutching the floor of the van, was in a situation he had never encountered and was not prepared for.

As I drove the van back, I was thanking God for making me bring the van out and not just walking to get Hunter. We arrived at the front picket fence gate. I would have to get Hunter out of the van and travel fifteen feet or so into the front yard. The horses were all around me; they couldn't control themselves. I jumped out of the van and grabbed a nearby aluminum ladder. Holding it over my head, making my self as *big* as possible, I screamed and the horses backed off, enough for me to toss the ladder, hit the van remote, and grab Hunter. I almost dragged him into the relative safety of the front yard. *Big mistake!*

Five daunting stairs loomed in our path to the house. They proved to be four too many for Hunter's shaking legs to handle. His legs fell out from under him on the second stair and he slid to the grass, just under the glare of the horses. I sat with him for about ten minutes and hoped he would catch his breath and get up the stairs. He didn't. I grabbed my cell phone and tried to call my sister's house. She or Paul would be here in a moment's notice. My neighbors' number came up. No, no, I wanted my sister's number! Again my neighbor's number came up. This time I smiled and said out loud, "Okay, I get it, God," and pushed the call button. "Hunter's in trouble!" Becky just said, "I'll be right there." Almost instantly I saw the dust rising from the gravel road. Becky just looked at the situation and asked, "What do you want me to do?"

"Calm Hunter as I get the back gate open, then scare the horses away so I can get Hunter in the backyard."

Becky is a genuine horse lady, and though we have had "issues," she loves Hunter. With her running cover and distraction, I got Hunter to the backyard (Harri in close attendance) and into La Quinta Lobo for some R & R.

I told Becky thanks and that steroids were in order. She looked at me, asked if I needed anything else, and said "BioFlex, just as good, easier on him, and over-the-counter at Walmart" then drove off.

Hmmm. That I could start today! I hopped in the van and headed for Walmart. I better pick up a box of her favorite wine as a thank-you. That evening when I returned home, Hunter looked well rested, calm, and happy to see me home. We all went inside as I watched him negotiate the three back stairs. He was stiff but made it look fairly easy. I laced a hot dog with a full dose of BioFlex. Again in the morning and again that night and next morning! I stopped by the vet, and he said to continue the BioFlex for six weeks. It *should* take that long to be in full effect! Wow, Hunter was showing improvement after three doses. By Tuesday morning he was happy again and not looking "old and sad." Becky was right, and Hunter and I were happy.

If Joe Louis knew, he might still be champ.

HC 57: THEY SAID SHE WAS OUT THERE

How many of you have heard this one? "Don't worry, you'll find someone." I hate that! I have Hunter, Harri, and Scat. Outside the house there are the horses, donkeys, and goats. Oh yeah, and Axle the llama. I have a great people photographer whom I see, and we photograph things. She's really wonderful, a young budding model who has worked with us, and we've gone to rodeos, concerts, and baseball games. She's lots of fun but about one-third my age. A real cowgirl who loves to shoot and ride and she's fun. A wonderful lady who works with the blind and we share a meal and conversation about once a month. A lady who wants me to teach her photography and she's cool. This should be just fine!

My friends, however, keep up the tribal chant "You need a woman in your life!" *A*, as in one who is everything to me. After three failed marriages and one long-term relationship, pretty much it must be me, so that's not going to happen. These days, being a Christian isn't unique, but praying directly to God and not attending a circus every week is. So when my close friends were "chanting" one night, I held up my hand and proclaimed, "If God wants me to have a woman who will be my best friend and soul mate, he will put her right in front of me, and I will know it." Well, that slowed the war drums, and the evening rolled along and ended with me going home to the crew.

Hunter was howling as I headed for the pen. Harri barking (like a dog does), Scat watched it all from the front deck stairs. The stars were insane, so we all sat on the back deck in wonder of the heavens. We did this a lot, and this is when my prayers pour out, usually thanking God for my many blessings.

Now, you do have to picture this—Harri lying down, Scat pacing as cats do, but Hunter and I staring at the incredible Texas night sky. Last thing I said out loud was "Oh yeah, and that woman thing, work on the Middle East. It'll be easier!" Hunter leaned over and kissed me. Weird. We all went in. I fixed treats for everyone, played with family, and went to bed with a happy "pack."

The next day, around 11:00 a.m., I was passing the Wells Fargo Bank and remembered that I had recently sold a property, and last time the title company didn't pay off the loan for six weeks! I had been funded, but had the mortgage been paid off? I was way ahead of my schedule, so I would just stop in and check, wouldn't take a minute.

As I walked into the bank, I was in visual shock. All four tellers had bags on their counters. Commercial accounts at all stations? A line "on deck" was fifteen deep. I walked up behind the last person in line and muttered to myself more than *to* anyone. "My god, how long is this going to take?" The last person in line was an impeccably dressed very petite (at least from behind) lady. She half turned around (no, I could not see her face) and said, "Well, I've had to shave my legs twice so far!" What? Did I hear that? I injected, "Well, if you hold my place, I'll go buy more razors for you."

She and the lady in front of her laughed audibly, but her laugh was amazingly pleasant and genuine. That's when it started, a banter from me and this lady's, ah, well, the back of her head! After a few minutes, the lady in front of her turned around and said, "Are you two here as entertainment for the rest of us?" Several others turned around and smiled. At one point I had said, "I hope my hair is still in style when we get out of here." The lady just turned around and said, "Too late!" She had me at "Too late." The twinkling eyes were amazing; her smile was childlike. I guessed her to be about forty and hauntingly pretty, but that was physical; her aura was bright and almost overwhelming. We chatted and smiled, and I tried desperately to glimpse at her left hand, but her eye contact was intense, and I didn't want to be caught.

Now the time in line was quick, too quick, and all of a sudden, we were too close. The lady in front of Jenny turned and winked at me. Hmmm. Then Jenny was called up, and it hit me like a ton of bricks. A ton of bricks that were *right in front of me*. I was called and I spoke very quickly, and the transaction was over and as I was ready to get the "zero balance" statement. Jenny waved and walked out the door. I grabbed the paper and almost ran to the door.

There, standing on the sidewalk, was Jenny. I casually walked through the door as if I hadn't a care in the world. She held a cell phone to her ear in her left hand. Her left hand with *no ring*! I had to be twenty-five years her senior, but I had to try. "Excuse me, but I really enjoyed that conversation in there, and if you did, would you like to continue that conversation over a lunch this week?" I was handing her my card and she was handing me hers. "Where I come from, the man does the calling," she said with that childlike smile. How did we *know* it was okay to exchange cards so boldly?

After a few lunches and a hockey game (yep, our favorite sports are boxing and hockey!), she asked to meet Hunter. "If he doesn't like me, I'll know there's no sense in dating."

The conversations were amazing, but she was correct. We *needed* Hunter's approval. He acted differently with everyone he's ever met, so this would be interesting.

I told Jenny to sit on the sofa and wait for Hunter's approval. Wolves are skittish with almost everyone, but if you've read the chronicles, you know that. I went out to the pen and let the big baby loose. By the time I caught up with him, he was sitting up on the sofa next to Jenny, just gently kissing the side of her face. As I write this, we've been "an item" for fourteen months, and every day I truly "know" we were meant to be together. I guess the reason the Middle East is still in turmoil? I guess God liked my challenge. By the way, Hunter sleeps with Jenny when she stays over!

Jenny has also introduced Hunter to Danish and his *crazy* new favorite, M&M's.

Thinking she was in her "early forties," I was shocked. Here she is sixty-one years old!

HC 58: THE CHRONICLES—WHERE DID THEY COME FROM?

About six years ago, I had the state of Alabama added to my sales territory. Whenever I get a territory addition or change, I visit everyone who has purchased anything in that new territory. I had traveled Alabama in 1974 with ARP synthesizers, but a lot has changed. I went to McCalla, a small town in 1974, but now, really almost a suburb of Birmingham. I followed the GPS as it led me to the address. Strange. I saw no shopping center, no giant sign, so I checked the list. Beanstalk music should be here. I then noticed that up a long driveway was a colorful Yellow House–type building with green shutters. Yep, that looks like a place named Beanstalk! I parked the car at the end of the driveway and smiled to myself. I love the music industry. Entering the green house, I noticed a collection of instruments unlike anything in your average music store. Turtle shell ukes and cigar-box guitars, I fell in love. The owner, Shirley Cates, then greeted me warmly, and we began to get acquainted. At one point she asked about me, you know, the who, what, why, and where in my life. When it got to animals (everyone who lives on a ranch has animals), I talked on about them and got to Hunter. She asked the usual questions. "Aren't you afraid?" "How did you domesticate him?" And of course, "How did you get him?" I basically told her the story of Hunter chronicle 1, and she posed a proposition. Can you write that down exactly as you just told me? Now you have to know that I have regretted not keeping a diary about Hunter, and this question was interesting. She asked me to write a new story every month for her newspaper. Her "other" business was a local paper (the *Tanne Hill*

Trader, later the *Leaf*). The stories would keep people picking up the paper and help her increase circulation. It was also a way for me to build a diary about my many experiences with Hunter. She asked me to e-mail her the first story, and she would "let me know."

Fifty-six chronicles later, I have my diary, and Hunter has a huge following in the state of Alabama. I think it has been a great adventure and my way of changing some attitudes about wolves.

Hunter is fifteen years old now, and that too is interesting. From what I've been told, wolves like Hunter's parents, living in a zoo, their life expectancy is three to five years! In the wild, we think the average is ten to twelve years, but honestly still very little is known about wolves in the wild. However, and here's the shocker, in a human home with love, a purpose, and nobody growing up to fill their place in the pack's hierarchy, seventeen to twenty years! That made me so happy to hear. Hunter has some aches and pains, but at sixty-five, so do I. He's had a few operations to remove benign tumors, but his vet says he has the teeth and vitals of a 5 year old malamute. Good news. When Shirley e-mailed and said "Let's do a reprint," I was excited all over again. We can add and edit chronicles and update everyone on Hunter's life.

He just had a couple large tumors removed, and his "haircut and stitches" were pretty bad looking, but a week later, he was playing like the puppy he thinks he is.

Again, thank you, Shirley.

VOLUME 8
ISSUE 7
OCTOBER
2012
Tannehill
Trader
An Alternative Publication with a Hometown Appeal
2nd Annual
Beanstalk
Music Festival
OCTOBER 6th 2012
LIVE ON STAGE!

HC 59: IT WOULD HAVE MADE A FUNNY PHOTOGRAPH HAD I NOT BEEN CRYING

I had just fed Harri and Hunter their evening polish sausage with Osteo-Bi-Flex in Hunter's portions. He always paces a bit afterward for some strange reason. I never question his rituals. There he was, sitting with his legs stretched out on the tile floor, forming a large V shape. It is the same position I sat in when playing marbles in elementary school. It would have made a funny photograph had I not been crying.

Hunter's now fifteen and a half years old, and the only sign of age is hip dysplasia, and it is getting worse. My first border collie (Buffy) had it starting around her seventeenth birthday. Her feet would slide out from under her, and she would scream and cry. The vet recommended steroid shots, one every six weeks. Yes, they do shorten the dog's life, but I wasn't concerned with longevity. Who would choose to have an animal that is suffering suffer for a longer period of time? The result was that Buffy played like a puppy, again chasing her beloved tennis ball endlessly. About five weeks later, she would begin to show signs of fatigue, then another shot and she was young again. This went on for three years till one day, she lay down, staring at the pool, and went to sleep for the last time. Three years of joyfully playing with no pain, which for Buffy was indeed forever. She was, in the words of Bob Dylan, forever young.

Tomorrow at 9:00 a.m., June 18, 2016, I will take Hunter in to see my vet for his first steroid shot. I hope it provides Hunter the same results that Buffy had. I love him dearly, and I want to do what is best for him. The vet and I have discussed this decision for almost a year now. He said I would know when to start the shots, and I do. Hunter has fallen a quite a few times recently, and last night it was three times, my heart breaking with each fall. I know it's been hard on Hunter, not chasing donkeys anymore, not running to the pond and swimming for a while in the bright Texas sun. These days, when I see Hunter asleep and his legs twitching in dreamland, I never wake him up, because in his dreams he still runs the ranch and plays in the fields. God willing, in a week he may capture some of that "Hunter" again. I certainly hope so.

Well, I often forget how little is known about wolves and what I should explain. Here goes wolf 101 life span: As was my luck, I bought Hunter from Arbuckle Wilderness (a drive-through zoo in Oklahoma). Well, in a zoo, a wolf's life span is between three and five years. I know what you're thinking; their spirit is removed and the children in the pack sold off to other zoo-type facilities (or a crazy old musician like me). Wolves live for the pack with a much better social order than humans. The young ones observe the elders and learn and respect them. The alpha male (the pack's leader) must be obeyed at all cost. The beta wolf is the nursemaid, and that position is both coveted and carries a great deal of responsibility. (This is the role that Hunter has displayed since he was six months old). Only the alpha male and alpha female will mate. It is for life, and they will only procreate *if* there is abundant food for the pups. Then there's the omega, the scapegoat of the pack, and he eats last and usually gets blamed for everything (not unlike George Bush). *Sorry!* Regardless, wolves in the wild live from ten to twelve years (most researchers agree on this but studies continue). However, in a human family where there isn't another wolf vying for position in the ranks, where medicine and health care is available, where they can love and be loved, where the wolf feels useful and needed, fifteen to twenty years' life expectancy! During the life span of all wolves, they desire one thing more than most species—to play. Hunter has always been a "player of games" as well as his stuffed squeaky toys. He and Jagger would play for hours, and Harri (though he tires quickly) puts up a great sporting spirit. Now with Scat (a female *and* a cat), well, let's say the place is pretty active, and yes, Hunter kisses everyone when he comes into the house, every time he comes back in the house. By the way, the term "fearless wolf" isn't exactly true. They have fear, one big one for sure—being alone. Hunter need not worry. Everyone loves Hunter, even people that have never met him and have only read the chronicles. Somehow I know he knows and loves them too. Unfortunately, the steroids did not work.

In the last few weeks, my vet has begun shots of Adequan every ten to eleven days. Hunter is himself again, and even though it's drug induced, it makes him feel good, and that is what my duty to him is all about. We are cherishing every day, every meal, every night walk, even every tear we shed together.

HC 60: IS IT ALL OUT OF FOCUS?

Lately, I guess for the last couple months, I've noticed that my quick snapshot photos have been, well, not in perfect focus. Okay, what can I expect from autofocus? As I have often said, every picture I've ever liked, well, they all had one thing in common: they were all in focus!

So is it asking too much for an autofocus shot to *actually be in focus*? Well, they're close, real close, *but not*, not sharp as a tack in focus. Sometimes the two-hundred-yard shot of an egret with a 600 mm lens was. Wait, the grass in front of the egret is *tack on*! So was I screwing up? Did I set the focus point wrong? The lens was *sharp*! I could shoot the moon and stun my friends with "stellar" (no pun intended) detail in focus! *But* I used manual focus in "live view." A snapshot of Scat on the back fence set me wild. All I wanted was a crisp photo, and it was out of focus. Not a problem, said Bill Porter, owner of Arlington Camera. At the Texas PPA School, we'll have the Nikon people there *and* the Tamron and the Sigma people there to grill. Go for it, Rick. If you don't attend Arlington Camera events for any other reason (hard to believe because there are *many* reasons), go for the free cleaning of the body, sensor, and lenses. All done in hours and by the factory (Canon and Nikon techs)! Well, I dropped off my 2 D-800 bodies and set off on a mission to "grill the lens guys." I had them take the lens and shoot pics and compare, zoom in, and check to see focal points, change bodies and lens to *really see*! They are all really cool guys, and we worked and worked to find an answer. No answer! So as I was wrapping up the day, it hit me. Maybe the body? So I walked up to the Nikon guys. "Say, have you got any idea how a body could produce out-of-focus shots?"

"A good healthy hit could offset the focusing sensor."

"What? I baby my cameras, but there's a 'focusing sensor'? Where?"

"Just to the left, as you see it, of the mirror. And by the way, something could be in the way." And they all smiled. Apparently, they had a "private joke" going on. "What do you mean 'in the way'?" The lead tech starts laughing and says one of the bodies we cleaned today had weird long white hairs on it! (They all laugh.) This guy's body had *hair* on the focusing sensor! They all laugh again and stopped when I asked, "Was it a D-800?"

"Er, ah, yeah, why?" I said four words. "I have a wolf." And they lost control and laughed and laughed *and* told the story of "forceps with scotch tape to get the hairs." Well, it was such a great story, I shared it with the Sigma and Tamron people—and you!

HC 61: WHO LIKES SHORT SHORTS?

I always took a picture of Hunter and me together on my birthday. Most of the time, I was holding the camera out and using a wide-angle lens. But for this one I used a tripod and a timer. Fifty-plus shots later, I got a good one. It's amazing Hunter put up with my running back and forth.

When Scat entered our lives, I was just hoping for a sort of mutually assured destruction kind of peace. I had no idea they kids would actually grow to love one another. Harri's not all that trusting of Scat, but Hunter and she kiss a lot. It's just beautiful to watch them.

Scat should probably have her own diary of sorts. Whoever tossed her out at the end of my gravel road could have never imagined the bundle of joy they abandoned. One night while Jenny and I were cooking, one of my lower cabinet doors was open about an inch. You have to understand that open cabinets door is one of Jenny's pet peeves, and when she saw it, she had to push it shut. No sooner had the door been shut than the one to its left opened a bit. Jenny was irritated and intrigued. She walked over and shut door number 2, and yes, door number 1 opened! After an adult version of "whack a mole," I opened door number 3 all the way, and a dazed Scat staggered out! Jenny and I were laughing so hard, we had to sit on the floor with Scat for several minutes. I didn't capture that moment, but last night, I was getting my meal ready, and suddenly I was startled by a *loud crash*! As I turned around, this is what I saw—another cabinet adventure.

You've seen them, pictures and paintings of a wolf face in the woods, only half of the face showing, half hidden by a tree. Well, it's not a "one in a million" moment. It's actually quite common. Why? When a wolf plays, he does this to make everything he sees in focus! Focus is achieved by two eyes at a fixed distance, so one distance is *in* focus, but everything else isn't! By hiding one eye, the wolf has everything in focus, so he misses nothing! In the wild, it's usually a sign that the wolf feels threatened. But It's also used when playing, Hunter's "half face."

Scat and Hunter watching TV in the dark! Evenings are so special at the ranch, I often take things and moments for granted. Don't do that! Cherish and photograph everything you can so you can lovingly "review" them when they are no longer part of your life. This photo is almost "painting like."

Hunter wanted me to find a picture to post on the Facebook timeline for the Thanksgiving weekend. I hope you like the post. The photo isn't mine; it's by Pam Dance. The caption on his Facebook? Okay, I wrote it, but it's true: "I love, I love, I love turkey!"

It was the Fourth of July 2015, and Kathryn, Jenny's daughter, was caught in a scheduling conflict and had to work that Saturday. The answer was easy but involved Hunter meeting the smallest human he had ever met—Jenny's grandson, only twelve weeks old! How would he react to such a small and fragile child? We weren't sure, but Hunter had always been very protective of the children who had visited before. We *knew* everything would be perfect—a perfect new experience for all of us.

Jenny and Hunter have such a close relationship. This is communication!

Hunter loved and babied Jenny's grandson.

He just wouldn't stop kissing him during the two-day visit.

One of Hunter's favorite "events" is meeting new people. He has well over three hundred friends and family, and I suppose, to him they are all pack members. This shot was taken when I invited the Rowlett Photography Meetup Group out to see and photograph the ranch. *Everyone* fell in love with Hunter. He was so animated and happy to have so many come to visit him. He looks tired in this shot, because he is. Vet visit tomorrow.

My cell phone takes great pictures, but every time I try a selfie, something really horrible happens. In this case, several things went wrong, but Hunter's nose looks about the size of Nebraska!

The term *night walk* have become words that if I say them, Hunter reacts and he loves them. The shadows often look like a Bat-Signal. Scat kisses Hunter when he returns.

We used to do ninety-minute night walks, but these days it's more to keep Hunter's legs moving and exercised.

Thanks to everyone concerned with Hunter's health. Things were bad last Wednesday, but since then, he hasn't fallen once. He has gone for two night walks, gotten up on the sofa to sit or lie next to me numerous times with no problems. He has eaten well, and the shakes have gone away, and the amazing wolf stare and golden playful eyes have returned to my big buddy.

There were years and years when Hunter could fly, and I pray he still does when he dreams.

Can you just imagine? How upset I was when I came across this "article," January 15, 2015.

This is what I get this morning. What a croc.

Wolves are in the top 10 "worst" pets?

There are reasons why we domesticated dogs. Their wolf and coyote ancestors were too wild to live alongside humans. Wolves and coyotes are still wild. They act on their instincts. They hunt when they are hungry, play when they want to, and sleep the rest of the day. If they feel threatened, they will attack. They can kill a full-grown moose and sense the sickest animal in a herd, even when that animal shows no symptoms. Like large cats and bears, they are far from domesticated and cannot be trusted.

Wrong!

There was a scary night for Harri and me. It was about a month ago when Hunter was feeling his worst. I heard Hunter leave (go out the doggy door) around midnight. I lay in bed and thought about the options that I wished I had to comfort him. I drifted off pretty easily because it was the first cold night of the 2016 fall. Somewhere around 4:00 a.m, I woke, couldn't hear Hunter's low and slow snore, and turned on the light. He wasn't there, and Harri was wide awake. I got up and looked around the other rooms in the house. Hunter was not in the house. I grabbed a flashlight and headed outside in my slippers and little else. I searched the backyard, but there was no sign of Hunter. Finally, I shone the light toward the La Quinta Lobo. In the very back corner, I saw Hunter. Because I have read so many wolf stories, my heart sank and my eyes welled up with tears. When a member of the pack gets old and worn out, he often goes away from the pack on his own, to gracefully leave this world. As I approached Hunter, I kept calling his name. No response, more tears. I got in the pen and stared at Hunter. I saw the rise and fall of his immense chest. I couldn't handle this; I was not prepared. Then he stirred and looked at me like I was crazy. Of course, the night was clear, the vast star scape over our heads. Hunter just went camping!

I love Facebook. I post all the photographs I take, and there are a lot of photos! Sunsets are amazing here, and moon shots, star scapes, macro flower shots, and of course, the ranch animals. All the Hunter shots go to his page. I want everyone to see them, so I leave it all in public mode. Hunter has lots of friends, and every now and then, someone requests to be my "friend." I always ask "How *do* you know me?"

"My husband and I are from Canada. He is a photographer and loves your work. I am an animal lover and I tell everyone about your Hunter posts. We are from Alberta, Canada, but recently moved to Phoenix, Arizona."

Sure. My parents are Canadian, and she was so nice in her request. She began to comment a lot and we became familiar with each other. One day she messaged me that she and her husband wanted to fly to Dallas and meet Hunter. Really? So you're here for a trip and want to see Hunter? No, we're coming just to see Hunter. I said yes, they did, and it was amazing. Hunter's dad was from Alberta, Canada, as are my mom and dad. Maybe it was the Canadian connection, but the visit didn't feel like a "meeting." It was more like a family reunion, and I can't wait for them to return!

Jacques Girard photographs his wife, Mercedes, with Hunter. Finally, they met!

Tonight I got home shortly after 8:00 p.m. I grabbed some ham hocks from the fridge for Harri and Hunter. Harri, like any dog, immediately attacked the treat. Hunter lay down next to it for almost an hour. Finally, I lay down with him, and we played with the ham hock. He bit it then pushed it toward me. I rolled it back and forth, and he chewed it a while then stopped and kissed me. All variations of the theme. "I'm not starving, I have food, but Dad and I are having a treat together. He has his ham hock and I have his company." Yes, tears stream down my face. Of course, he's old too, and we are both mortal, but the overwhelming love needs to be passed on to those who only know dogs and cats. This bond is like no other I've even seen or read about. Tomorrow I will wake early so I can remove my bed frame. Hunter's legs are not allowing him to share my bed. I will remedy that, but for tonight I wanted you to know we are so happy.

In the summer of 2016, Hunter had a serious hip dysplasia. He wasn't really in pain, but he looked so confused. Steroid injections didn't work, and the next suggestion was Adequan. It's part painkiller, part cure. Hunter showed some improvement but not really much. His confidence was gone. I lowered my bed, or should I say "the" bed. On most nights Harri, Hunter, Scat, and I occupied the king-size bed and all was well, but Hunter didn't want to walk on the tile or wood floors or go for his night walks.

So after a couple months of this, I asked desperately what else I could do for him. "Well, we could try laser treatments," said the vet. "Let's do it," I said and never asked what the cost was. I didn't care. When I paid the bill after the first session ($150), I thought that was what each of the six treatments would cost. Well, I would have to rebudget some things, but he was my best friend.

After the second session, two things happened. Number 1 was the *best*. He regained his confidence almost instantly! I couldn't believe it. He wanted to walk again, and he actually hopped on the passenger seat after the fourth session. When I would pick up Hunter's leach, he would stretch and come to me right away, and he would hold up his head to expose his collar! Here we are driving home from session five. Look at that face!

Oh yes, number 2. The $150 turned out to be for all six laser sessions. I spent it on treats!

Of the thousands of photos of Hunter, there are only fraction of us together. Of all those, this is my favorite. Taken by a fellow photographer, Gene Duprey. He is fabulous at capturing, and capture he did. I hope you see it too, the loving bond between us.

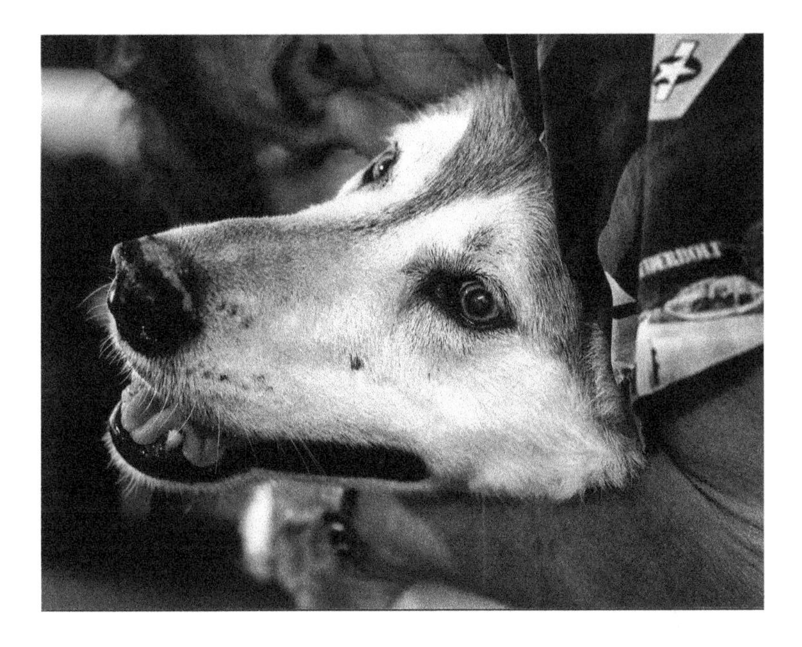

We play and cuddle every moment. When I work at the computer, he just stares at me. I love Hunter so much, and I love the life we've made for ourselves.

HC 62: YESTERDAY, TODAY AND TOMORROW

"From time to time, a man wonders, he thinks and realizes, really, that he is closer to the end of the journey than the beginning. He says to himself, 'What was the sum of it all?'" That's a paraphrase of Sir Alec Guinness in *The Bridge Over the River Kwai.*

But it's true. I'm sixty-six now, and Hunter is almost three times as old as the expected lifetime of a wolf in captivity. Wow. As I write this, he's on the floor near me, twitching his leg in some "wolf dream." One of the small prices you pay when you live alone is the lack of pictures of yourself. In my case, the price is that I have very few pictures of Hunter and me together. About six or seven years ago, we had had a great weekend, as usual, and I got my neighbor to take some photos of Hunter and me together.

I sent this one out, and someone noted that we look too much alike. Eyebrows, they said. Thank you. I love his "look." I feel we have grown closer over the years, and he has calmed me down as my cardiologist had hoped. I have evolved and arrived with his guidance at a peaceful place in God's world. I can only wish, pray, and suggest to you—try to travel here and stay as long as you need. I feel you will not want to leave.

I'd love to say that the Hunter chronicles are going to continue forever, but that's not true. In any relationship this close, someone has to bear the incredible weight, the loss of the other. My heart condition is getting no better, and Hunter is "pushing whatever" in wolf years. Like a fool, I continue to work full-time.

With the many life changes that have happened in these recent years, my time at home has increased dramatically. What a great gift from God, no matter the price or cause.

Hunter has taught me so many meaningful lessons about love and life. You get a pet and want to teach them tricks. His teachings are so much more spiritual. From the little guy he was to the big lug in this photo (him, not me), he has changed my soul and changed the lives of so many willing to listen to his stories. If you hear the gentle words of this wolf, you will be opened to the lessons of a lifetime—life lessons from another species.

I love him and he loves me, and nothing can ever diminish that. There will be additional segments till that fateful day, just not as regularly. I've shown pictures of Hunter to people and had them say, "Oh, I love wolves," and I think, you don't know. You haven't cuddled with one, comforted one, fed one, made a wolf "feel better" when he was hurt, cheered him up when he was sad, lifted him up when his legs were failing and he wanted to be on the bed next to you. You haven't had one howl to let you know where he was, that he missed a family or pack member, or walked side by side in the woods at night. You haven't tossed a meatball in the air and had a wolf snap it up and "grin" at you or had him "sneak" onto your bed and had a gentle kiss at 3:00 a.m. No. Many people "love wolves," but I am blessed by God above. I have a wolf that loves me.

EPILOGUE

It was early November 2016 when I received a Facebook message from the "No Kill" animal rescue in Quinlan, Texas. This is a wonderful place run by Dr. Alan Cadis, his wife, and several volunteers. He follows the Hunter chronicles on Facebook and had made up his mind to ask that I come in as an "expert." I've been called that (expert) several times in my life and it's not really a title because "ex" means former and "spurt" is a drip under pressure!

"We have 2 full blood wolves. One female is pregnant and we would love to have you show us how to socialize them." I was flattered and intrigued but I never socialized Hunter. If anything, he socialized me! Wolves are pack (family) animals, and there's no trick–they either accept you as family or they don't. They love you or they are afraid of you.

I sent off for a DNA Breed kit and gave it to Dr. Cadis and waited till I got the call a few weeks later. "Mom is 87% wolf and 13% unknown." That means she's a wolf and I asked to see her that Friday. "By the way, she had 6 pups on November 4th. Can you spend time with them?" What's the dad? "We think he was also part Lab." Part Lab? Better that Chihuahua but what was the "other part?" Well, it should make for an interesting morning, better show up at 7:00 AM.

On December 9th, a bitterly cold morning, I drove to Quinlan, Texas and met the mom Cheyenne and her female friend and nursemaid Faith. It was time to put on my "expert" hat.

Janice walked me to the special wolf enclosure and my jaw dropped–here were the 2 female wolves. The pups hadn't emerged from the "house" yet. I entered the enclosure, walked 5 feet from the back of the "house," sat down and waited. Cheyenne and Faith circled and watched me, getting closer and closer. The pups ran to Janice for the morning snacks she regularly brought. There was one that was particularly animated, stretching and greeting Cheyenne and Faith with kisses. She was a momma's girl but after a few minutes, she walked to the water bucket for a morning drink. After a drink, she looked up at me and just stared. What a cutie, I thought but those ears and that tail? She's got dog in her for sure. Another drink and another stare, a glance at mom and she walked to me.

I extended my hands and instead of sniffing or kissing she crawled into my arms. This one is a lover. She is going to make a wonderful … ah … hybrid? I stood up with her in my arms and she began cooing and moaning! She'll make someone a great family member. It was time to put her down and see the interaction of the other pups. As I loosened my grip on her, she screamed and dug her paw into my arm!

I could hear laugher. Janice "saw" the interaction and knew, I guess so did I. Janice asked, "What's her name, Rick?" Windy. It's short for "Windsong." That was the day that Hunter got a Granddaughter, Harri got a niece, I got a beautiful little lady and Scat? Hunter accepted her like a lost friend and relative. He let her cuddle up with him, sleep on his body and even play with his tail. He had a new purpose in life. Hunter would train this little family member in the ways of the ranch. In the first day, she was using the doggie door, drinking water from the water tank and "Wolfing down" Goat's milk.

That was 8 weeks ago, 8 fun filled weeks of a new family dynamic with a growing, really growing beautiful lady named Windy.

Last night after I fed everyone the nightly treats and ate my dinner while watching the ID Channel, I reviewed my difficult day. I needed a shower to wash off the day filled with disappointment and setbacks.

When I got out of the shower with the day washed off, I couldn't help but notice –Hunter and Windy had turned green! Now you have to know that earlier I cleaned my carry weapon. Afterwards I put the cleaning "stuff" back in the drawer. The drawer with some, well "boy toys" specifically 37mm Green Smoke Grenades. I forgot to close the drawer and there are children in the house. BAD MOVE! Hunter and Windy finally did something together as a team. They TRIED to look innocent BUT.... I watch a lot of ID Channel and I put it all together instantly! Laughing all the while, I see a new carpet in my future.

The moment was great. Windy and Hunter were at long last "partners" – partners in crime but still partners.

Love.... Floppy ears and all

Day one of Windy's ranch life

This is tolerance

Partners in crime

PICTURES

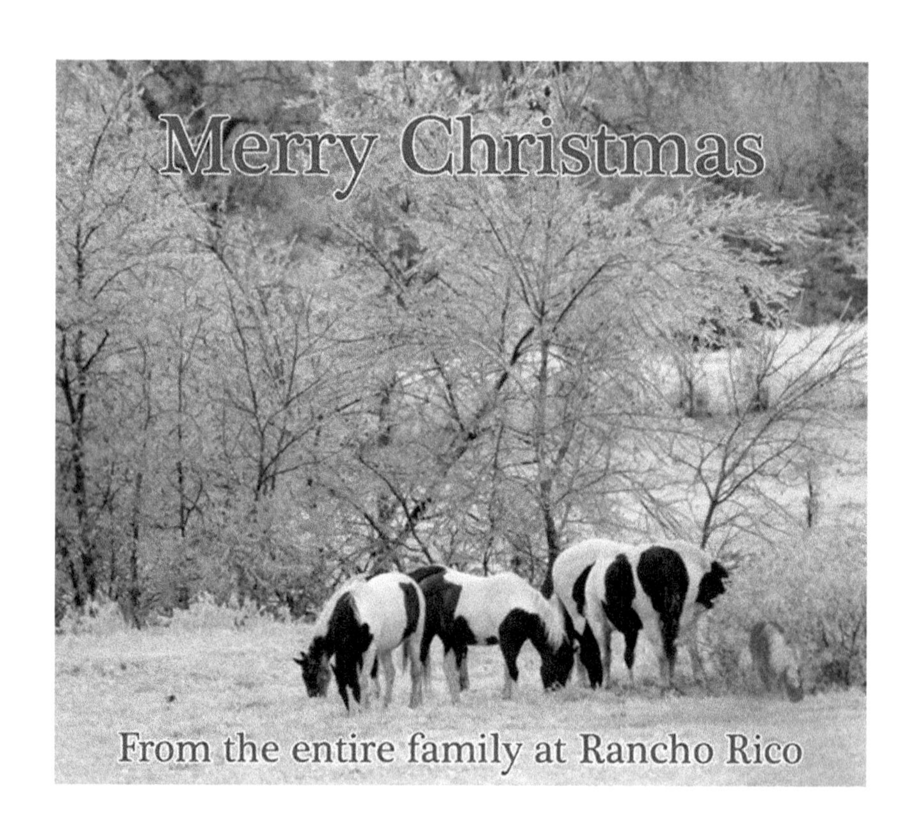
Merry Christmas
From the entire family at Rancho Rico

Le Bistro

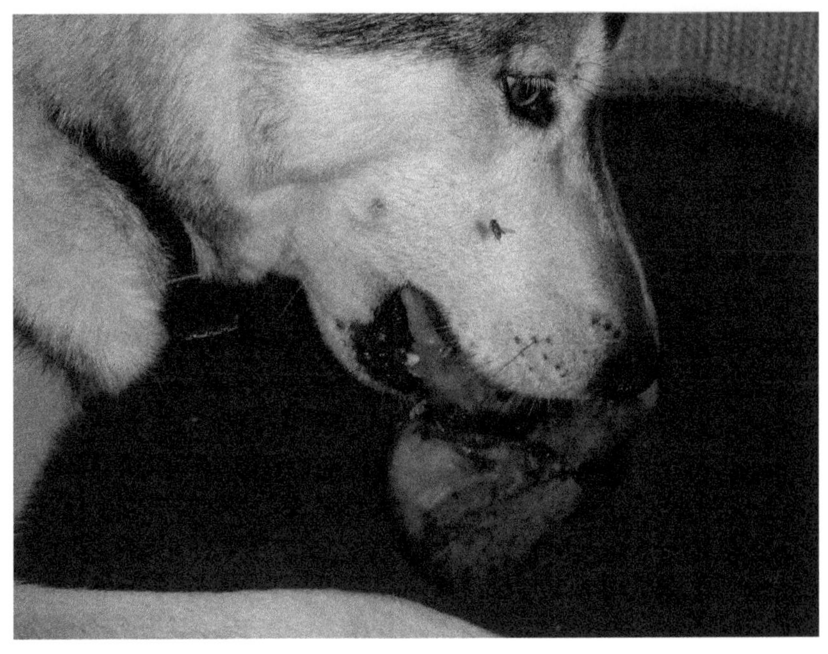

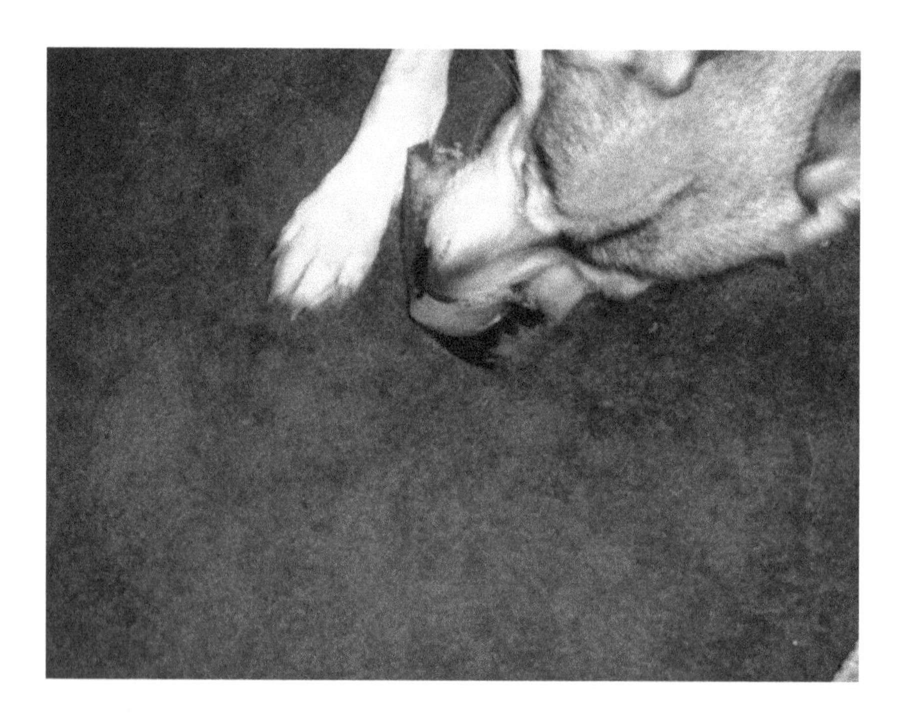

OTHER

Thank You

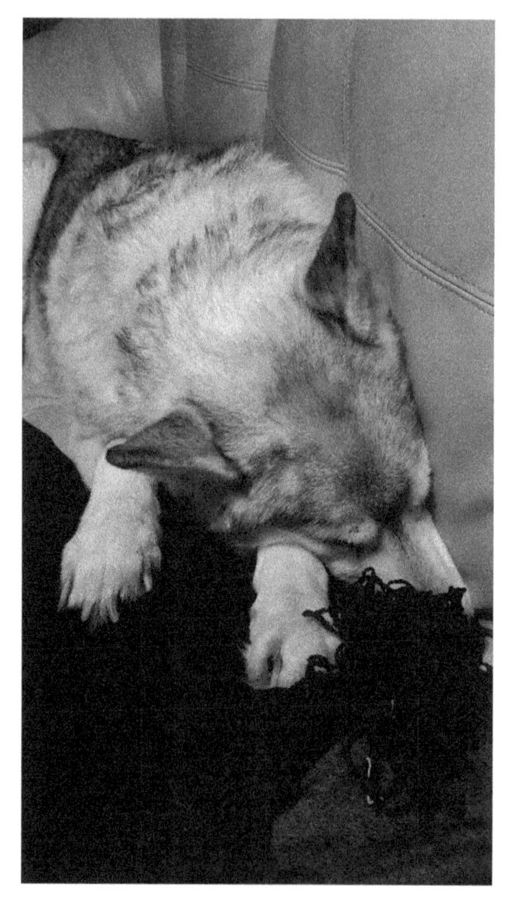

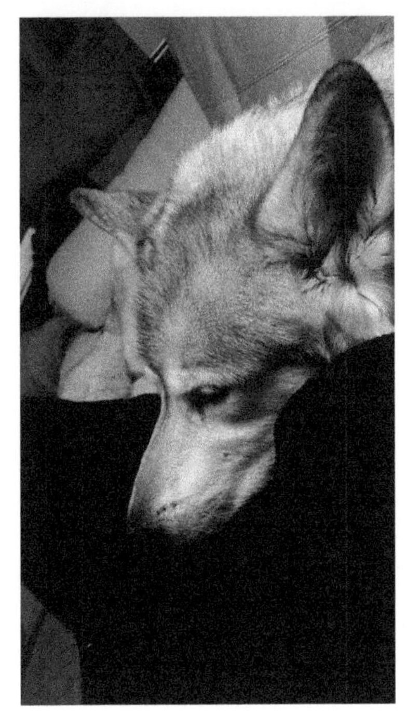

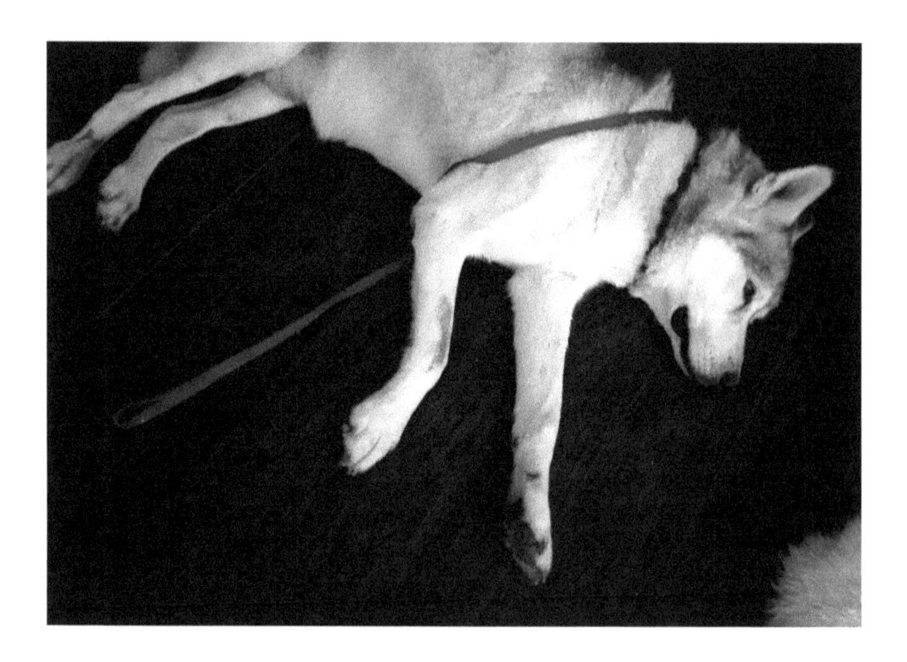

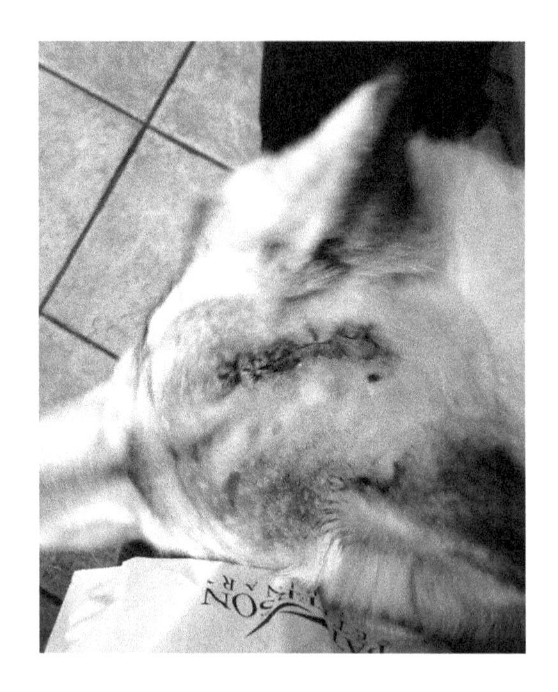

COMMERCE
VETERINARY
CLINIC
DR. GARY THOMPSON

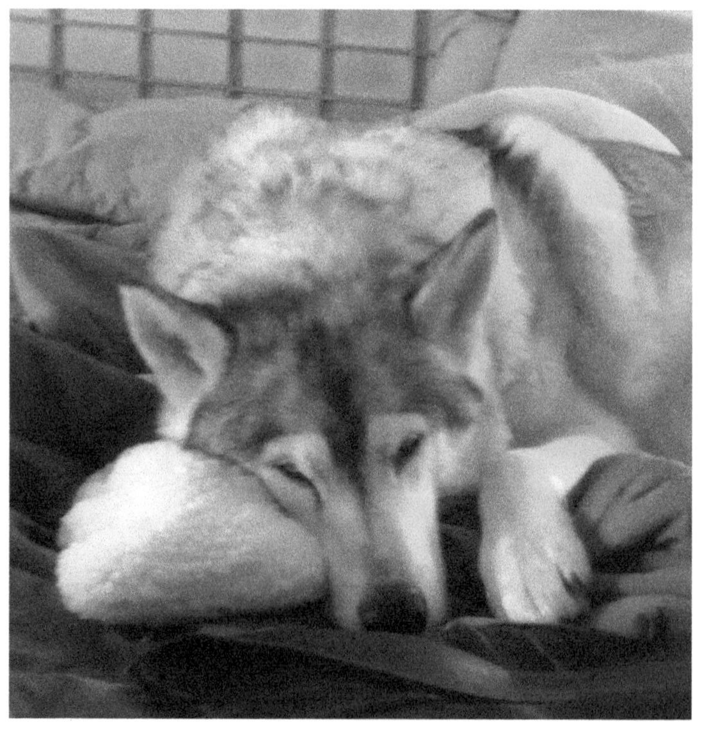

HUNTER

ABOUT THE AUTHOR

Rick Parent was born November 12 1949 in Miami Florida to immigrant parents. At the age of 10 his family moved to Washington D.C. Always in love with the music he spent over forty years in the music business. A Heart attack forced him to "de-stress" his life and he among other of the Doctor's suggestions he moved to the Texas countryside and lives on a 100 acre ranch with horses, donkeys Llamas and goats. As interesting as it is, the journey from the Night clubs of Washington D.C. to a small east Texas ranch is of little importance compared to finding his soul in the lessons from a wolf named Hunter.

Hunter passed away on August 5th 2017. A Lovely lady from New Orleans granted her daughter's life wish to kiss, pet and hug a real wolf. Hunter, always the gentleman sat with her and loved meeting them. He passed an hour after they left. He was 119 in K-9 Years.

Rick is now Managing Director of a school of the arts in Commerce, Texas. He helps under privileged youth with song writing and the fundamentals of photography.

Contact Information:
Rick Parent
PO Box 501
Commerce, Texas 75429
Rickparent2@aol.com

CPSIA information can be obtained
at www.ICGtesting.com
Printed in the USA
LVHW01s2119280318
571253LV00003B/4/P

9 781640 276024